Asset Allocation
DeMYSTiFieD®

Asset Allocation
DeMYSTiFieD®

Paul J. Lim

New York   Chicago   San Francisco   Athens   London   Madrid   Mexico City
Milan   New Delhi   Singapore   Sydney   Toronto

1 2 3 4 5 6 7 8 9 10   QFR/QFR   1 0 9 8 7 6 5 4

ISBN   978-0-07-180977-1
MHID   0-07-180977-5

e-ISBN   978-0-07-180978-8
e-MHID   0-07-180978-3

This publication is designed to provide accurate and authoritative information in regard to the subject matter covered. It is sold with the understanding that neither the author nor the publisher is not engaged in rendering legal, accounting, securities trading, or other professional services. If legal advice or other expert assistance is required, the services of a competent professional person should be sought.

—From a Declaration of Principles Jointly Adopted by a Committee of the American Bar Association and a Committee of Publishers and Associations

McGraw-Hill Education products are available at special quantity discounts to use as premiums and sales promotions or for use in corporate training programs. To contact a representative, please visit the Contact Us pages at www.mhprofessional.com.

Contents

chapter 1

What Is Asset Allocation?

Ask any pastry chef or baker: What would happen if you gathered together all the best ingredients in the world—vanilla from Madagascar, chocolate from Oaxaca, Échiré butter from France—but failed to take the time to mix them together properly? You'd end up with an expensive but decidedly disappointing dessert, right? Ask any construction worker: What would happen if you were to combine water, sand, and cement together, but in incorrect proportions? You'd most likely get a weak batch of concrete, and a potentially dangerous foundation for your structure.

In a nutshell, that's what asset allocation is all about. It is the process by which investors can build a safe, solid foundation for their investment portfolio by making sure not only that they own sound investments, but that those assets—ranging from stocks to bonds to cash to real estate to gold and other commodities—are held in the proper proportion based on their circumstances.

What Defines "Proper" Asset Allocation?

Should you invest for capital appreciation (a fancy way of saying growth) by loading up on assets that increase in value quickly? For instance, should you keep, say, 75 percent of your money in stocks, with 15 percent in real estate and 10 percent in bonds? Or should your goal be capital preservation (i.e., safety at all costs) by keeping all or most of your money in relatively stable investments—for instance, 50 percent of your money in bonds, 25 percent in gold, and 25 percent in cash?

There are a whole host of factors that go into answering this question and establishing what the proper mix of stocks, bonds, real estate, gold, and other assets is for you and your portfolio.

For starters, there are the variables you hear about most often from the personal financial media and the financial services industry: your age and the approximate year in which you intend to retire. In the parlance of personal finance, this is referred to as "your time horizon." These factors are indeed quite important. After all, you're investing for a goal, and for most Americans, the biggest goal is likely to be the ability to pay for a long and comfortable retirement in the future.

> *A Key Fact to Consider:* The more time you have before you'll need to spend the money you're investing, the more risk you can afford to—and should—take with your portfolio. Often, that means the greater exposure your portfolio ought to have to stocks, especially fast-growing shares.
>
> This is true not only because a person with a long time horizon can afford to take more investment risk, since he or she would have time to make up for any short-term setbacks the portfolio might suffer early on. It's also because time has a funny way of eroding the value of anyone's portfolio through the deleterious force known as inflation, which chips away at the purchasing power of one's money over time. And over extremely long periods of time, the compounding effects of inflation every year can really put a dent in your portfolio (Table 1-1).

Personal Sensibilities

You cannot ignore other variables that are more personal—that speak to who you are as an individual and what your circumstances are now and could be in the future. For instance, how would you describe yourself as an investor? Are you a risk taker by nature, or do you feel more comfortable playing it safe? What is your psychological tolerance for risk? When faced with unexpected bad news, are you likely to double down your resolve and stick to your guns? Or are you much more likely to panic at the earliest signs of bad news?

TABLE 1–1 Loss of Spending Power *Over time, inflation can eat away at the future purchasing power of your nest egg.*			
Today's Dollars	**10 Years**	**20 Years**	**30 Years**
$100,000	$73,700	$54,400	$40,100
$200,000	$147,500	$108,800	$80,200
$300,000	$221,200	$163,100	$120,300
$400,000	$295,000	$217,500	$160,400
$500,000	$368,700	$271,900	$200,500

All of this matters in establishing the right investment strategy for you, because the worst thing you can do is set forth an investment plan early on—for instance, one that requires you to be heavily weighted toward stocks, and not just any equities, but the riskiest types of shares, such as those of a tiny start-up—that you know in your heart of hearts you'll ignore or upend down the road when the pressure is on (for instance, should the stock market run into a hiccup or a sustained downturn).

Financial Circumstances

There's also your fiscal tolerance for risk: your financial ability to withstand any setbacks that you may encounter throughout your investing career. In other words, how much money do you really have to work with? This question would seem to make sense: If you're single and have no dependents, your financial needs would be much lower—and your ability to take risk would be much higher—than those of a married person with four kids and a spouse who did not work.

If you have a rich uncle who you know will leave you a considerable estate that's big enough to pay for your entire retirement, than you can afford to take risks with your own portfolio because if push comes to shove, you won't need it to live off. By contrast, if you have no safety net to fall back on—if there's no inheritance, no family assistance, and you expect little in the way of Social Security and other benefits—then what you do with your own portfolio of stocks and bonds will really matter. And you can't afford to take any undue risks with it.

A Key Fact to Consider: The more money you have to work with, the more risk you can afford to take. This is exactly opposite to the assumption that many investors make. There's a commonly held belief that if you are far behind in your savings and need to make up for lost ground, you should "roll the dice" by overweighting risky but fast-growing assets in hopes of rapidly growing your pot of money in a short window of time. Call it the lottery approach.

Yet the laws of math say that if you have a small pot of money to work with, you have little flexibility to be taking much risk at all. Instead, you should concentrate on preserving what little you have in your portfolio while working to make up ground in other ways—for instance, by saving at a faster clip or finding a way to boost your income in the short term.

On the other hand, if you are sitting on tremendous amounts of wealth, you can actually afford to take risks with your portfolio because: (a) you have sufficient funds to fall back on if things were to go awry; (b) if you were to fall short of your ultimate investment goals, even earning a modest return on a large sum of money can still generate a sizable income for you; and (c) if your wealth is a by-product of a sizable annual salary, you can afford to replenish your losses through savings, recovering quickly from any market losses.

The list of variables that affect your asset allocation strategies doesn't stop there. There are other considerations you have to factor into your decision making, such as your family finances (which speaks to your financial options), your own health (which speaks to the potential length of your retirement and your potential retirement income needs), your spouse's health, and your employment and income stability.

So there is no perfect asset allocation plan that you can look up on a computer. There are a variety of strategies, though, that can offer you the right balance that over the long run, will deliver the types of returns that you crave while exposing you to only that level of risk that you can tolerate, given who you are and your circumstances.

Why Asset Allocation Matters

The sad truth is, many of the factors that help you determine your asset allocation strategy often go unconsidered from the get-go. In fact, asset allocation is among the most important decisions that investors all too often overlook. Most people spend the bulk of their time and energy on trying to select the absolute best individual securities, be they stocks, bonds, mutual funds, or exchange-traded funds.

At first blush, this would seem to make sense. After all, who doesn't want to know what the next Google or Apple will be? Knowing that information before others do—and placing bets based on that knowledge—would be like winning the lottery.

But individual security selection is just one component of several that go into investment success. In addition to which stocks you ultimately select, another important factor is *when* you choose to buy those securities. There's also when you ultimately choose to sell those investments to book the actual gains. There's also knowing which securities to avoid so as not to suffer losses elsewhere in your portfolio. There's also minimizing fees and other expenses to keep as much of the market's returns as is possible. And then there's the recipe by which you ultimately mix those individual investments in order to create a solid financial foundation for your portfolio.

Now, you may be wondering: Isn't it unfair to compare the recipe for a pastry and a portfolio? For instance, if three-quarters of a cake were made up of sugar and only one-quarter of flour, you'd have a sweet mess on your hand. On the other hand, if three-quarters of your portfolio consisted of a stock that gained 50 percent in value every year, you'd love to have such a sweet mess on your hand, wouldn't you?

A Key Fact to Consider: Even seasoned stock pickers can't consistently select stocks that outperform the broad market over time. The financial firm Standard & Poor's routinely analyzes the performance of professional mutual fund managers compared with the broad stock market indexes that they're paid to beat.

Their recent analyses uncovered something unsettling: Over the past five years, less than a third of the pro stock pickers who specialize in large blue chip stocks managed to beat the Standard & Poor's 500 index of large blue chip shares, the benchmark that measures the performance of equities that make up most of the market's total value (Table 1-2). Worse still, less than 25 percent of all mutual fund managers who specialize in picking small-company shares managed to beat the S&P 600 index of small-capitalization stocks over the past five years, even though that's what they're paid to do.

Indeed, if you were smart enough to choose only the best stocks in the world, those that are destined to double and redouble in value over time, what does it matter if they represent 25 percent or 75 percent of your portfolio? In either case, your money would grow, right? Fair enough.

But the answer to this question boils down to a couple of factors. First, there's the reality check of being able to select only investments that are destined to grow in value. It is true that if you had the skills and luck to be able to select only moneymaking investments, asset allocation would not matter a bit. In reality, though, no one makes money consistently on *all* of his or her investments.

TABLE 1–2 Most Professional Investors Fall Short
Percentage of mutual funds that failed to beat their benchmarks.

Fund Type	Benchmark	Past 1 Year	Past 3 Years	Past 5 Years
U.S. Large Caps	S&P 500 Index	85.5%	85.2%	65.4%
U.S. Small Caps	S&P 600 Index	91.0%	83.9%	77.7%
U.S. All Caps	S&P 1500 Index	92.2%	85.3%	76.2%
U.S. Real Estate Stocks	S&P U.S. REIT Index	85.3%	90.0%	72.6%
Global	S&P Global 1200 Index	66.0%	73.1%	61.6%
Foreign	S&P Foreign 700 Index	54.3%	66.1%	73.7%
Emerging Markets	S&P/IFCI Index	50.3%	66.4%	83.7%

Data through June 2012. *Source:* S&P

Even the absolute best stock investors don't bat a thousand when it comes to their own portfolios. For instance, Reynolds Blue Chip Growth ranks as one of the absolute best-performing stock funds in recent years, having posted annual gains of more than 13 percent over the past five years when competitors barely eked out average returns of 3 percent. In fact, Frederick Reynolds, the manager of the fund that bears his name, outperformed 99 percent of his peers during that stretch. Yet a recent look at his fund's holdings showed that about a quarter of his top 25 picks had actually lost value in early 2013. This doesn't detract from Reynolds's skills as an investor. It simply means that he, like every other investor on the planet, is human.

The results are even more pronounced among amateur investors. Dalbar, a financial consulting firm that tracks investor behavior, determined that over the past three years, the average stock fund investor underperformed the broad equity market by more than 3 percentage points a year (Table 1-3). Similarly, the average bond fund investor underperformed the broad fixed-income market by more than 3 points on average per year. Over the long run, the results are far worse. Over the past 20 years, the S&P 500 index of stocks gained roughly 8 percent a year on average. By comparison, the typical stock fund investor earned barely half those gains annually on his or her investments.

That may not sound like a big difference. Over time, though, it adds up. Had you invested $10,000 at the start of each year for the past 20 years and earned 8.2 percent on your investments, you'd have amassed nearly $468,000 by now. If, on the other hand, you earned just 3.5 percent on the same investments, you'd be sitting on a portfolio worth just $307,000. That's 35 percent less thanks to the power of compound interest.

TABLE 1–3 Most Individual Investors Also Fall Short
Amateur investors routinely underperform the markets too.

Time Period	Investor Returns in Stock Funds	S&P 500 Stock Index	Investor Returns in Bond Funds	Barclays Aggregate Bond Market
Past 3 Years	7.6%	10.9%	2.9%	6.2%
Past 5 Years	–0.8%	1.7%	1.6%	6.0%
Past 10 Years	6.1%	7.1%	1.2%	5.2%
Past 20 Years	4.3%	8.2%	1.0%	6.3%

Data through 2012. *Source:* Dalbar

A Key Fact to Consider: No investment consistently rises in value day in and day out over time. Even if you defy the odds and have the ability to find only the best stocks in the world, you're still not assured of being a successful investor. Think of history's most astounding equities—Apple Computer in the 2000s, Microsoft in the late 1990s, Coca-Cola in the 1980s. Each stock has had its fair share of rough patches that lasted in some cases months if not years.

Indeed, Apple is the biggest stock in the world today, with a market value of nearly $500 billion. Yet between 1990 and 2003, the stock's price actually declined in value. Similarly, Microsoft remains one of the most successful stocks in the market's history, having achieved a market value of more than $500 billion in the late 1990s. Yet between 2000 and 2012, the stock's price has declined.

So the question isn't simply the stocks you pick. Your success will also depend on the timing with which you buy and hold those shares. Yet history shows that individual investors almost always underperform both the broad stock market and professionally managed mutual funds because we tend to be late to identifying investment trends or are impatient and sell before seeing investments fulfill their potential (Table 1-4).

TABLE 1–4 Investor Returns *Individual investors also underperform their own funds by bad timing decisions.*		
Fund	**Fund Returns Past 5 Years**	**Investor Returns Past 5 Years**
Vanguard Value	7.9%	4.8%
Fidelity Contrafund	8.0%	6.2%
American Funds AMCAP	10.1%	7.5%
Dodge & Cox Stock	7.6%	4.5%
T. Rowe Price Equity Income	8.3%	7.2%

Source: Morningstar

How Much Does Asset Allocation Matter?

In recent decades, there's been considerable academic debate about how important asset allocation really is to your long-term success as an investor. At one point, in 1986, three finance professors published a controversial study that determined that more than 90 percent of the variations of returns generated by funds were actually due to the mix of assets they held, not the underlying investments. This was followed up by later studies that questioned the accuracy of that original finding. Some believe that when it comes to determining the actual level of returns that a fund generates, asset allocation can explain closer to 100 percent of the results.

This all sounds astonishing, and hard to believe, since this would mean that one's stock-picking decisions play almost no role in one's investment success. But let's be clear. Those studies were based on the practices and results of professional mutual funds that are sold to the public. And professional mutual fund managers have an obligation by law to be "diversified." In other words, a professional money manager is almost always likely to hold a diverse mix of stocks that represent a big chunk of the broad stock market. In the mutual fund industry, this is sometimes referred to as "closet indexing." The term simply refers to the fact that a fund manager whose job it is to invest in, say, U.S. stocks is likely to own shares that represent the majority of the market value of the U.S. market.

In that case, the proportions with which professional investors mix their holdings are likely to be extremely meaningful, since they would be one of the few things that differentiate them from their peers as well as the market itself.

Individual investors, on the other hand, are under no legal obligation or professionally mandate to own most of the stocks in the market. In fact, some investors may choose to own only a handful of shares. And if you own only five or six different stocks, than stock selection will matter a great deal.

Still, in an age where you can get broad market exposure through professionally managed mutual funds or even a basic S&P 500 index fund, there's a decent chance that you have broader exposure to the overall market than you may think. So your asset allocation decisions can still have a big impact on your investing results.

Why Investing Matters

Investing—that is, putting money to work in stocks, bonds, real estate, or other assets such as commodities so that it appreciates in value over time—used to be someone else's problem. That was when the bulk of workers used to receive some combination of a guaranteed pension from their employer and Social Security checks to fund their retirement income.

When that was true, about a generation ago, investing was important to the pension fund managers who were responsible for cutting retirees their monthly checks. Yet it mattered little to individuals, most of whom stayed clear of the financial markets until at least the 1980s and early 1990s.

Thanks to a wave of reforms instituted by cost-conscious corporate executives, though, that all began to change about two decades ago. In the late 1980s and early 1990s, companies began to off-load the risks—and costs—of investing pension money onto their workers. To compensate, policymakers and the financial services industry gave rise to a collection of self-directed retirement accounts such as 401(k) plans (for which you're eligible via your employer) and IRAs, individual retirement accounts that workers could establish on their own through banks, insurance companies, and mutual fund companies.

These tax-deferred savings accounts help individuals amass their own nest eggs from which they can draw income upon retiring. However, any mistakes or inefficiencies they encounter as investors throughout their working years will directly cost them in their golden years by leading to smaller account balances and, in turn, a more modest monthly income. In the past, such mistakes and investment shortfalls due to pension manager error were simply covered by the company, as pensions come with explicit promises of guaranteed levels of income. There are no such guarantees when it comes to a 401(k) or IRA. In effect, the burden of risk has shifted: It now falls squarely on the shoulders of American households.

At the same time, the money that households receive from Social Security is covering a smaller and smaller portion of their retirement income needs. When the Social Security system was first created in the 1930s under the Roosevelt administration, Social Security would cover the bulk of one's retirement income needs. Today, the payouts, for a typical upper-middle-class family, might only cover a quarter to a third of one's needs (Figure 1-1).

Part of that is due to demographic shifts taking place in the country. But it also has to do with the fact that Americans are enjoying a retirement that's significantly longer—today's 65-year-old can reasonably expect to live at least 25 to 30 years—and higher in quality than their parents and grandparents could ever expect (Table 1-5).

Yet to maintain that type of fulfilling and comfortable retirement, the onus is on you to invest your money in a sufficiently effective manner that requires basic knowledge of how portfolios work—and how sound asset allocation can make those portfolios work better.

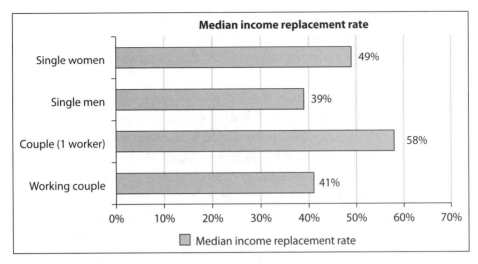

FIGURE 1–1 Social Security
Social Security covers less than half of many households' preretirement income.

Source: Center for Retirement Research

TABLE 1–5 The Long Road of Retirement			
Life expectancy based on specific ages			
Men who make it to this age...	**...can expect to live to this age**	**Women who make it to this age...**	**...can expect to live to this age**
55	80.2	55	83.6
60	81.3	60	84.3
65	82.5	65	85.2
70	84.0	70	86.3
75	85.9	75	87.8
80	88.1	80	89.7

Source: Social Security Administration

What You'll Learn from This Book

This book is geared for individuals who don't necessarily know all the ins and outs of investment theory, but who know that they'll need to invest at least well enough to secure their own future. Each chapter is designed to walk you through the basics. For instance, in Chapter 2, you will get a basic understanding of the underlying principles behind diversification along with the basic assumptions surrounding asset allocation strategies. In Chapter 3, you'll get the lowdown on the key risks and rewards of the major ingredients that go into your asset allocation strategy.

Then the book switches gears and focuses on setting your own strategy. In Chapter 4, you'll learn how to determine what the most appropriate mix of stocks and bonds is for you. Then in Chapter 5, you'll find ways to elaborate on that theme by allocating within your stocks and bonds. You'll see how those model portfolios have performed, in terms of both risk and reward, in recent years.

In Chapter 6, you'll learn about the different types of adjustments you can make with your strategy. Using cash, dividend-paying stocks, and alternative assets such as gold, real estate investment trusts, and commodities, you'll learn how to make tactical shifts and "tilt" your portfolio to further customize your strategy to meet certain goals, such as fighting inflation and seeking income. You'll also learn how to take advantage of hidden premiums found in certain types of stocks. Chapter 7 will discuss some alternative approaches and theories to retirement investing that aren't part of the mainstream of personal financial dogma just yet, but that are gaining more and more attention. Then in Chapter 8, you'll learn the importance of periodically resetting your mix of stocks and bonds back to your intended mix, because failing to do so can quickly upset your plans. Finally, Chapter 9 lays out the various ways you can automate your asset allocation strategy so that you don't have to obsess over it over time.

Hopefully, whether you choose to hand those decisions over to the pros or manage your asset allocation on your own, you will find enough information in this book to answer your key questions, pique your interest, and get a feel for constructing the strategy that's best suited to you.

QUIZ

1. **Asset allocation is ...**
   A. More important than individual security selection.
   B. Just as important as individual security selection.
   C. Less important than individual security selection.

2. **Asset allocation is designed to boost your portfolio's ...**
   A. Risk.
   B. Returns.
   C. Risk-adjusted returns.

3. **Asset allocation matters because investors are ...**
   A. Skilled at selecting individual securities.
   B. Unskilled at selecting individual securities.
   C. Uninterested in selecting individual securities.

4. **The key to establishing the right asset allocation for you is knowing ...**
   A. What type of investor you are.
   B. Which types of stocks are likely to beat the broad market.
   C. Whether stocks or bonds are due to outperform in the future.

5. **Investors who are skilled at picking stocks and funds need asset allocation ...**
   A. Less than those who are unskilled at picking stocks and funds.
   B. More than those who are unskilled at picking stocks and funds.
   C. The same as those who are unskilled at picking stocks and funds.

6. **The more time you have to invest, the more your portfolio needs ...**
   A. Stocks to stay ahead of inflation.
   B. Bonds to stay ahead of inflation.
   C. Stocks to stay ahead of bonds.

7. **The less time you have, the more you need to turn to ...**
   A. A big stock allocation.
   B. Individual stocks.
   C. Bonds.

8. **The less money you have, the more you need ...**
   A. Bonds to preserve what little you have.
   B. Stocks to make sure that the little money you have grows over time.
   C. Neither.

9. **The following factors matter to your asset allocation strategy:**
   A. Your age
   B. Your risk tolerance
   C. Your wealth
   D. None of the above
   E. All of the above

10. **The more your portfolio is diversified, the ...**
   A. Greater the impact of asset allocation.
   B. Greater the need for sound stock selection.
   C. Less the importance of asset allocation.

chapter 2

The Underpinnings of Asset Allocation

At the core of asset allocation is a simple principle: You're always better off with a diversified portfolio that holds several different types of investments at the same time rather than a concentrated portfolio with just one asset in it, let alone a single security. Translation: Having many eggs in your proverbial nest is better than having a single fragile one.

That's because it is simply impossible to know with certainty which investments will make the most money and which will lose the most in a given stretch of time. So by having at least some exposure to all of the basic asset classes at all times, you're assured that at least some portion of your portfolio will be in investments that are thriving at any given moment in time.

There is, of course, a downside to this approach. Diversification also means that you're assured of having some of your money in lagging or poorly performing assets at all times, too. That's the price you pay for hedging your bets in exchange for a little peace of mind. Think of diversification, and in turn asset allocation, as an insurance policy that you buy. In exchange for giving up the possibility of maximizing your potential gains to the greatest degree possible, you obtain assurance that you'll never experience the worst possible outcome at any given time in the markets.

Consider that since 1926, a 100 percent stock portfolio has returned around 10 percent a year, which is great. Plus, in 52 of the past 86 years, stocks were the absolute best-performing asset class available to investors. Even better. Yet there have been years along the way in which equities have lost value—sometimes a great deal of money. In all, stocks have fallen in 14 out of the past 86 calendar years, and in their worst 12-month stretch, the equities dropped about half in value.

Now consider what happens when you add just one layer of diversification—in this case bonds—to that all-stock strategy. Yes, the average annual performance drops, since bonds are slower-growing assets than equities. A portfolio that was half invested in equities and half in bonds has returned 9 percent annually since 1926, not 10 percent. But for that 1 percentage point reduction in expected returns, you get a noticeable drop in risk.

The average half-stock/half-bond portfolio has lost money in only 9 of the past 86 calendar years. While it's never been the best-performing strategy in any calendar year, it's never been the worst either. Moreover, this balanced strategy reduces your volatility—in other words, the day-to-day ups and downs that all investments expose people to—pretty much in half (Figure 2-1). And instead of losing around half its value in the worst-ever year for the financial markets, this diversified portfolio lost less than a quarter of its value in its worst 12-month stretch.

While embracing diversification doesn't sound like a controversial idea, it actually runs counter to the thinking of some of the world's most famous investors.

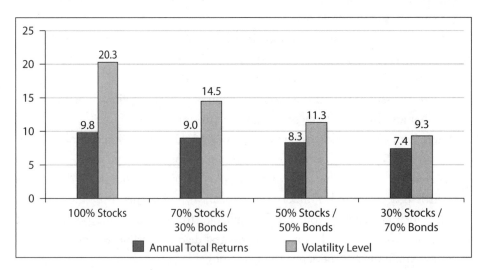

FIGURE 2–1 Risks and Rewards
Adding bonds to your portfolio will reduce your returns, but also your risk.

Source: Ibbotson Associates

Warren Buffett, for instance, once proclaimed, "Diversification is protection against ignorance. It makes little sense for those who know what they're doing." This helps explain why the mutual fund industry is constantly creating "concentrated" portfolios, which focus the bulk of their assets in only a handful of the fund manager's favorite or supposed best ideas. Of course, history shows that funds that concentrate their bets don't necessarily perform better—in fact, there's a good deal of evidence that shows they perform worse. Over the past decade, stock funds that spread their bets among 100 or more individual securities have outperformed those that concentrate their assets in 30 or fewer stocks (Table 2-1).

TABLE 2–1 Diversification Wins *Stock funds that spread their bets outperformed concentrated portfolios.*	3-Year Annual Returns	5-Year Annual Returns	10-Year Annual Returns
100 + Stocks	17.7%	8.7%	8.7%
31 to 99 Stocks	16.4%	8.0%	8.2%
Less than 30 Stocks	15.3%	8.2%	8.2%

Source: Morningstar

Buffett would further clarify his remarks by implying that diversification is for amateurs. Well, if you're Warren Buffett, you can make such a statement. But the 99.9 percent of the rest of us are, in fact, amateurs when it comes to investing. There's no shame in saying that. The vast majority of us don't invest full-time. We work. We have families. We have outside interests, leaving us with little time to manage our portfolios minute by minute, day in and day out.

Even professional money managers who work in the same field as Buffett—and who invest full-time—can't lay claim to having successfully beaten the market consistently over long periods of time. What's more, even Buffett himself can't lay claim to always outperforming the market. In the three-year period ending in June 2013, for instance, Buffett's investment company Berkshire Hathaway returned 12 percent annually, which was more than 6 percentage points worse than the broad stock market. And in the five-year period ending June 2013, Berkshire Hathaway produced annualized gains of less than 7 percent, which is just a hair less than what you could have earned simply by putting your money in a basic off-the-shelf S&P 500 index fund, which many big mutual fund companies sell (Figure 2-2).

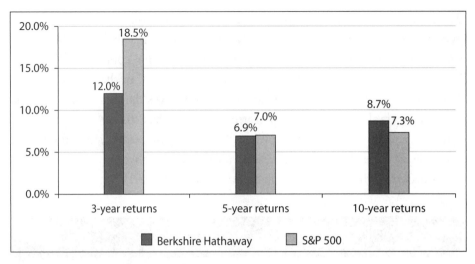

FIGURE 2–2 Berkshire Versus the Market
Even Warren Buffett can't always beat the markets.

Data through June 30, 2013. *Source:* Morningstar

Predicting Asset Performance in the Short Run

Over any one-, three-, or even five-year period, it's nearly impossible to tell how certain assets will behave. For example, in the global financial panic, U.S. and European stocks were expected to fall, since the housing meltdown in the developed world directly affected consumers and banking institutions in those regions. The emerging economies of China, India, and Brazil, on the other hand, weren't directly impacted by the credit crisis, and their economies continued to grow rapidly even when the United States and Europe fell into recession. Yet in 2008, when the U.S. stock market lost around a third of its value, Chinese stocks lost much more—they fell by nearly half.

In 2009, a year into the crisis, U.S. corporations suffered an epic earnings collapse brought about by the Great Recession. With the economy in tatters, U.S. firms had trouble selling their goods and showed a huge quarterly loss. Meanwhile, the consumer economy took a big blow as the nation's unemployment rate more than doubled to 10 percent that year. Yet in 2009, American equities soared nearly 27 percent.

While conventional wisdom says that key factors—such as the health of the economy, the fiscal health of the government, the growth of corporate earnings, and the profit margins that businesses enjoy—ought to drive the performance of stocks, over any short period of time, that's really not true. Researchers at the Vanguard Group, an asset management company, tried to learn how various fundamental factors such as GDP growth and corporate earnings affect the stock market over time.

They came to a rather surprising conclusion. Over a one-year time frame, these factors had zero predictive power over the future direction of equity prices (Figure 2-3). Over a one-year time horizon, there is simply no correlation between economic or earnings signals and future stock performance. "In fact," the report concluded, "many popular signals have had a lower correlation with the future real return than rainfall—a metric few would link to Wall Street performance. Broadly speaking, our results here are consistent with several academic studies that have documented the difficulty of forecasting stock returns."

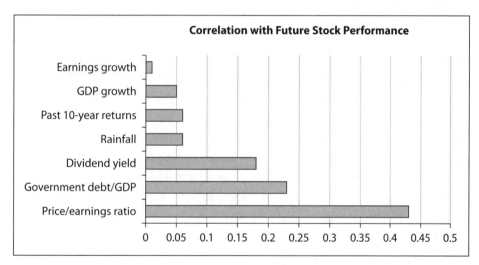

FIGURE 2–3 Predicting Stock Behavior
1.0 implies strong predictability; 0.0 implies no predictability.
Source: Vanguard

Predicting Asset Performance in the Long Run

While stocks, bonds, and other assets are difficult to forecast over any short-term period, in the long run they're actually quite predictable. We know, for instance, that stocks and bonds come with certain return expectations given the amount of risk they've historically exposed investors to. We also know that while in the short run, stocks and bonds can deviate significantly from those historic norms, the market's hidden hand eventually pushes those assets back in line with their average returns. This force is called "reversion to the mean."

The financial markets are like a pendulum. While there may be periods when investors, for whatever reason, drive a particular asset up or down to historic extremes, the price change will eventually alter the valuation on that investment so much that investor opinions about it will shift. This could take years. An asset class may be in favor or out of favor for nearly a decade—for instance, the Internet stock bubble in the late 1990s, and the housing bubble in the early to mid-2000s. But eventually, investors will overreact in the other direction, and over time, the asset will be back in line with its historic average performance.

The most recent example of this took place with U.S. stocks. From the start of 2000 to the end of 2009, U.S. equities did something they rarely do—they lost money over a 10-year stretch (remember, they've historically averaged gains of around 10 percent a year). This was why this period is frequently referred to as the "lost decade" for Wall Street. By 2009, stocks sank to their lowest valuations in more than two decades. That, however, drove money back into equities, and after a bull market that more than doubled equity values from 2009 to 2013, stocks wound up posting average annual gains of nearly 9 percent from 2003 to 2013.

Reversion to the mean can sometimes take more than a decade to occur, so you have to be patient. But over the long term—meaning the next 10 to 20 years—you can expect your various assets to perform largely as they have for much of history. That means stocks are likely to generate greater returns in the long run and greater losses in the short run. True to form, while equities have beaten bonds in only 60 percent of the calendar years since 1926, they've outpaced fixed income in 83 percent of rolling 10-year stretches in that time and in 96 percent of the rolling 20-year periods (Figure 2-4).

Different Asset Classes Take Turns Leading the Market

Asset allocation would not be necessary if any single category of investment led the market for several years straight. If that were true, it would be easy to excel at investing—you'd simply observe which investments were posting the best results at the time, and then you'd ride the momentum for four or five years. Of course, it's never that simple. The fact is, even in times when stocks are beating bonds or vice versa, different types of equities and fixed income take turns posting the market's best gains. It happens in almost every year.

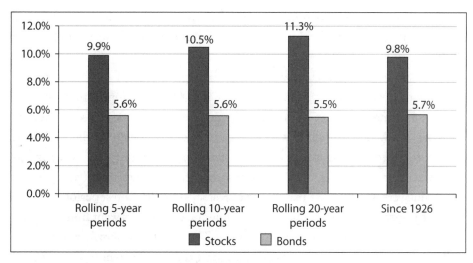

FIGURE 2–4 Stocks Versus Bonds over Time
Over the very long run, equities have historically outpaced fixed income.
Source: Sasdfkd: Vafaf

Take a look at Table 2-2. What you'll see is that the best-performing investment in 2012 were real estate investments trusts. The year before that, it was U.S. bonds. Two years before that, it was small-company stocks. Before that, it was foreign fixed income. And the year before that, it was commodities.

TABLE 2–2	Asset Rotation *Investments take turns leading the market.*	
	Top-Performing Asset Class	**Worst-Performing Asset Class**
2012	Real estate investment trusts	Commodities
2011	Long-term Treasury bonds	Commodities
2010	Real estate investment trusts	Cash
2009	Small-company stocks	Cash
2008	Global bonds	Foreign stocks
2007	Commodities	Real estate investment trusts
2006	Real estate investment trusts	Commodities
2005	Commodities	Global bonds

Source: MFS

In other words, there was no way to predict the optimal place to invest, and asset allocation got around this problem by holding on to these asset classes at all times.

Just as significant is the fact that one year's best-performing asset often turns out to be among next year's worst—and vice versa. In 2008, for example, amid the worst of the global financial crisis, U.S. Treasury bonds were one of the few safe havens in the global market. Any investor who was scared about the health of the worldwide economy dashed into Treasuries to see shelter from the storm. Well, when things started to improve in 2009, Treasuries went from the best performer (with gains of 26 percent, versus a loss of 37 percent for U.S. stocks) to the poorest performer (with losses of 15 percent). At the same time, emerging market stocks went from last place in 2008 (with losses of 50 percent) to gains of 72 percent the following year.

By diversifying your assets across a broad spectrum of investments, you avoid the worst-case scenario: being whipsawed by rapid turns in the market. A common mistake that investors make, for instance, is selling out of an asset after the market crashes, and then sitting out of the same asset when the market is bouncing back.

Diversification May Fail You

One thing that asset allocators concede is that diversification doesn't work 100 percent of the time. Under normal economic circumstances, different asset classes will move in different directions and at different speeds. In an economic or financial crisis, though, all bets are off. When fear is the dominant emotion moving the markets, there's a good likelihood that assets that expose investors to economic risk (for instance stocks, corporate bonds, and high-yield bonds) are likely to fall in unison.

That was certainly the case in 2008, when U.S. stocks, foreign stocks, emerging market stocks, commodities, and junk bonds all lost value at the same time. That year, researchers at Ibbotson Associates looked at the correlations between different asset classes, such as U.S. stocks and foreign shares. They found that in months when the markets gained value—presumably in relatively stable economic times—the correlation between the Standard & Poor's 500 index of U.S. stocks and the MSCI EAFE index of foreign shares was a modest 0.31 (a correlation of 1.00 would signify that two assets move in perfect lockstep with each other).

However, Ibbotson researchers then looked at the correlation between U.S. and foreign shares in months when the stock market lost ground (presumably during periods of higher anxiety in the economy and the markets). In those months, the correlation jumped to a reading of 0.53.

The same thing happened in the relationship between U.S. stocks and emerging market shares. In up months, the historic correlation was 0.24, which implies very little relationship between the two. But in down months, that correlation spiked to 0.59.

Just because two investments move in the same direction in a crisis, though, does not mean that diversification has completely failed. For example, in the bear market of 2002, U.S. stocks lost more than 22 percent of their value. That same year, foreign stocks in general, and European and Asia-Pacific stocks specifically, also lost value in lockstep with the United States. But European shares fell 18 percent that year, while Asia-Pacific equities lost 9 percent. That means that if you were diversified among the three regions—with, say 60 percent of your stock portfolio in the United States, 20 percent in Europe, and 20 percent in Asia—your total equity holdings would have lost 18 percent of their value that year, not the full 22 percent by which U.S. shares dropped.

Under Most Circumstances, Diversification Works

While globalization has recently increased the overall correlations between asset classes, there is still a statistically significant difference in the behavior of asset classes in general and among asset classes in the United States and abroad. For example, the historic correlation between foreign and U.S. stocks is 0.7, which is still well shy of the 1.0 correlation that would imply that two asset classes move in unison.

Ibbotson approached this question from a different angle. Researchers at the firm studied the difference between annualized returns for U.S. shares and foreign stocks on a rolling five-year basis going back to 1970. In theory, if the world has grown so interrelated that diversification is becoming irrelevant, then the difference in annualized five-year performances for U.S. shares and foreign stock would be virtually negligible. The two sets of returns should ride the same line.

Yet U.S. equities posted significantly higher returns in the late 1970s and early 1980s, significantly worse returns from the mid-1980s to the late 1980s, significantly higher returns in the 1990s, and then significantly worse returns in the mid-2000s.

And don't forget that between the major asset classes—in other words, stocks and bonds—correlations remain extremely low, making diversification as relevant as it has ever been (Table 2-3). The historic correlation between U.S. stocks and

TABLE 2–3 Correlations Between Investments
A reading of 1.0 means assets move in lockstep.

	International Stocks	Large-Cap Stocks	Small-Company Stocks	Long-Term Corporate Bonds	Long-Term Government Bonds	Intermediate-Term Government Bonds	Cash
International Stocks	1.00						
Large-Cap Stocks	0.66	1.00					
Small-Company Stocks	0.50	0.72	1.00				
Long-Term Corporate Bonds	0.04	0.28	0.11	1.00			
Long-Term Government Bonds	–0.12	0.06	–0.10	0.89	1.00		
Intermediate-Term Government Bonds	–0.14	0.08	–0.08	0.88	0.89	1.00	
Cash	0.00	0.10	0.04	0.00	0.00	0.30	1.00

Source: Ibbotson Associates

long-term government bonds, for example, stands at a mere 0.06, according to Ibbotson. This would explain why, in 2008, when just about every stock market in the world fell in lockstep, Treasury bonds generated 26 percent in total returns. So if you had a diversified mix of 60 percent U.S. stocks and 40 percent Treasuries that year, your overall portfolio would have fallen a mere 12 percent in 2008, despite the fact that equities dropped 37 percent.

The Markets Are Largely Efficient

The universe of investors can broadly be divided into two camps: On the one hand, there are those who believe that the markets are inefficient—and that information regarding individual stocks and securities is incomplete and/or misunderstood. If that's the case, individual investors who have more information than their peers and who have the wherewithal to process that information more astutely should, in theory, be able to make more money than the market over the long run by picking better investments.

On the other hand, there are plenty of investors who believe that the markets are for the most part efficient. In other words, in this digital, democratized age, all the important information about any given stock or investment in the marketplace is pretty much known by the market as a whole and by most discerning investors. Therefore, individuals have little chance of consistently "beating" the market through superior security selection. The long, dismal track record of professional fund managers trying but failing to beat the market over the long run seems to attest to that.

Proponents of asset allocation fall into this latter camp. Since it is difficult—if not impossible—to gain an advantage through better research or analysis of individual securities, the idea is that investors shouldn't even try to pick their way to success. Efficient market theory holds that you can't beat the market over the long term through superior stock selection. The only way to outperform the broad market is to expose your portfolio to greater risk in a manner that is likely to generate higher returns. And that is accomplished by altering your mix of asset classes, not by attempting to pick the very best securities in each asset class.

Investors Care About Risk as Much as Return

Ultimately, asset allocation strategies assume that individuals care about more than just maximizing returns. If all investors focused on was just earning the biggest possible gains, then investing would be simple: Just load up on equities, especially the riskiest types of stock. Over the very long term, the odds are decent that you could come out ahead with this approach. That's if your portfolio managed to survive losses in the short run, because such a strategy would stand to lose a lot in routine market downturns and bear markets.

Instead, asset allocation theory assumes that investors behave rationally. And rational investors care about maximizing the amount of return they can earn based on a set level of risk—often the level of risk that they can afford. For example, if you know that you cannot afford to lose more than 20 percent of your portfolio value in any downturn, than your goal would be to find a strategy that delivers the greatest potential return while at the same time theoretically limiting your losses to that level. If riskless Treasuries held to maturity were delivering higher returns than this theoretical portfolio, then a rational investor would go with the riskless option. If not, the investor would opt for the diversified allocation strategy.

As such, there are several ways investors must think about risk. Obviously, the potential losses that an investment can expose you to—and the likelihood and frequency of those losses—is at the most basic level a very real risk that you must be mindful of. You need to know, under the worst circumstances, how much money you could lose with various asset classes.

But risk is much more nuanced than that. For starters, investors must always be mindful of volatility—that is, the tendency of an investment to move up and down in price on a regular basis. Because volatility is a single measure that gauges both potential gains and losses, it is a useful way to think about investment risk.

But how do you measure volatility? Investment volatility should be gauged in at least two dimensions. For starters, there's something called **beta**. Beta refers to how sensitive an investment—be it a stock, a fund, or an asset class—is relative to movements in the broad market (Figure 2-5). The beta for U.S. stocks and stock funds would be measured against the S&P 500 index. The beta for foreign stocks might be compared against the MSCI EAFE index of foreign stocks.

If a stock fund were to have a beta of 1.20, that would mean that it is roughly 20 percent more volatile than the broad stock market. In other words, if the S&P 500 index were to fall 1 percent on a given day, you would expect this stock investment to fall 1.2 percent. Conversely, if the market were to rise by 1 percent, you would similarly expect the investment to gain 1.2 percent. This is an important type of risk to measure because often, investments don't just rise or fall based on the individual circumstances of the underlying company. Sometimes investments move because the rest of the market is either rising or falling. The lower the beta

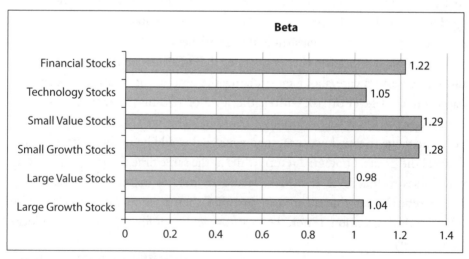

FIGURE 2–5 Investment Risk—Beta
A beta of 1.2 means an asset rises or falls 20% more than the broad market.
Based on 5-year averages. *Source:* Morningstar

of your portfolio, the less it is likely to fall when the broad market does, and the less market risk you expose yourself to.

The broad market isn't the only force that can drive your individual investments up or down. Sometimes, the price of a stock or stock fund may fall because of the inherent volatility in the investment itself. This type of risk can be gauged by a statistical measure called **standard deviation**.

In the simplest terms, standard deviation speaks to the steadiness of an investment by looking at its volatility relative to its own average performance over a set period of time (Figure 2-6). So stocks, with a standard deviation of around 20, are considered volatile because if you were to plot out the historic performance of equities over time, the distribution of plot points would be fairly wide. By comparison, government bonds have a standard deviation of about 10, which signifies that the historic range of all bond market performance is about half as wide. True to form, over five-year periods since 1926, stock performance ranged from as high as gains of 29 percent a year to as low as annual losses of 12 percent. The range of intermediate-term government bonds' performance was far tighter. In the best five-year run, government bonds gained 17 percent, and in the worst five-year period, they gained 1 percent.

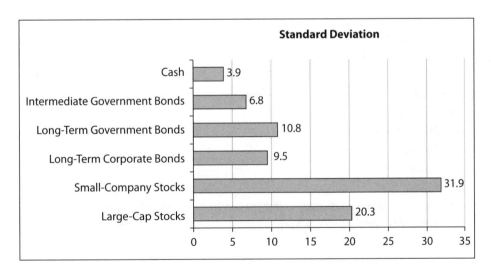

FIGURE 2–6 Investment Risk—Standard Deviation
The higher the reading, the rockier an investment is.

Based on long-term historic averages. *Source:* Ibbotson Associates

QUIZ

1. **Asset allocation assumes that diversification ...**
   A. Always works.
   B. Never works.
   C. Mostly works.

2. **It is impossible to determine the short-term performance of investments.**
   A. True
   B. False

3. **It is impossible to determine the long-term performance of investments.**
   A. True
   B. False

4. **Which of the following fundamental factors can influence the direction of stock prices over the short term?**
   A. GDP growth
   B. Corporate earnings
   C. Profit margins
   D. None of the above
   E. All of the above

5. **Investments tend to revert to their historic performance over ...**
   A. 1-year periods.
   B. 5-year periods.
   C. 20-year periods.
   D. Never.

6. **If the market is truly rational, investors can boost their returns by ...**
   A. Increasing their exposure to risk.
   B. Increasing their exposure to stocks.
   C. Improving their stock selection.

7. **If two asset classes always move in the same direction, diversifying between them is pointless.**
   A. True
   B. False

8. **In an age of globalization, asset allocation is …**
   A. Less important.
   B. More important.
   C. Just as important.

9. **Standard deviation measures an investment's volatility relative to …**
   A. The stock market.
   B. A broad market benchmark.
   C. Itself.

10. **How much is an investment with a beta of 1.5 likely to rise if the broad market climbs 1 percent?**
    A. 150 percent more
    B. 50 percent more
    C. 5 percent more

chapter 3

The Building Blocks of Asset Allocation

There are two core assets that are considered the basic building blocks of asset allocation: **stocks** and **bonds**. In this chapter, we'll explore both assets in detail.

Your Stocks

Stocks are often the first thing people think of when they consider investments.

What They Are

When you buy a stock, you are literally buying a stake in a business. That's why stocks are also referred to as equities, because shareholders have a literal equity stake in the company whose publicly traded shares they hold.

Now, you may only own 50 or 100 shares of a particular company, and that firm's ownership may be split among 10 million or 100 million shares. So from a voting standpoint, you have little sway over the direction of the company, its management, and even its dividend policies. Nevertheless, because you are a part owner of a for-profit institution, you are a recipient of the potential rewards and real risks that come with owning your own business. Which is to say, things can go very well for you (think Google's stunning rise in the 2000s or Microsoft's dominance over PCs in the 1990s), or alternatively, things could go very wrong (think Enron filing for bankruptcy in 2001 or WorldCom following suit in 2002).

Why You Need Them

So why are equities considered such a critical building block for any investor? Simple: Ownership of a company's shares is distinct from owning any other asset in the world. Unlike gold or silver or real estate or cash or industrial commodities such as oil, a business has the potential to grow. Not just to grow in value, based on what investors collectively deem it to be worth. Businesses can literally grow in scale based on the decisions of the executives who run the firm and the board of directors that oversees them.

For instance, had you bought shares of Walmart when it first sold stock to the public in 1970, you would have been signing on to a largely regional U.S. consumer company with fewer than 50 stores and sales of less than $80 million a year. Today, Walmart isn't merely a successful seller of general merchandise in the United States; it is a multinational retailing giant with more than 10,000 stores spread among 27 different countries, employing 2.2 million workers globally and with nearly $500 billion in annual sales. Moreover, it's not only the world's biggest seller of dry goods—it also happens to be the biggest grocery company out there.

Now, not all companies are like Walmart. Some grow only modestly every year, while others don't grow at all. A number, in fact, go out of business at some point or are sold off because of the failures of their executives and the vagaries of the economy.

That said, over long periods of time, equities on average have been shown to create more wealth, in real inflation-adjusted terms, than any other asset class (see Figure 3-1).

Therefore, stocks juice your portfolio with the potential for long-term capital appreciation that helps you literally grow your nest egg even after the deleterious effects of inflation, which again is the erosion of the purchasing power of your dollars over time.

Indeed, since 1926, stocks in general have delivered annualized gains of about 10 percent, at a time when inflation rose only about 3 percent a year. What does that mean? It means that if you were to invest $10,000 a year in stocks every year

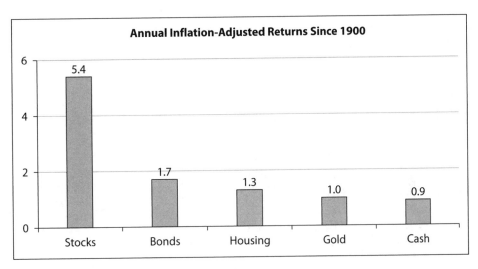

FIGURE 3–1 Real Returns
Over time, stocks have typically delivered the biggest returns on an after-inflation basis.

Source: Credit Suisse

for the next quarter century, and if equities continue to deliver the same general returns as they have for nearly a century, your investments would grow to more than $1 million in nominal value, assuming that 10 percent rate of return. Even after inflation's long-term effects, your money would, a quarter century from now, be able to purchase about $690,000 worth of goods.

By comparison, bonds have posted annualized long-term gains of less than 6 percent over time, again versus a 3 percent average rate for inflation. Now, that may not seem like a huge difference from the stock market's performance. But if you were to invest that same $10,000 a year in bonds returning slightly less than 6 percent, your nest egg would grow only to slightly more than $500,000 in that same time in nominal terms. And after inflation, you'd really only be able to buy about $365,000 worth of goods and services with that nest egg. That's a $325,000 difference in real purchasing power by investing in stocks over bonds.

The difference in the real long-term earning power between stocks and cash is even starker. If you invested $10,000 a year in cash—which has historically gained about 3.6 percent a year over nearly a century—you'd amass only about $269,000 in inflation-adjusted terms, which is less than half what you'd get with equities (Figure 3-2).

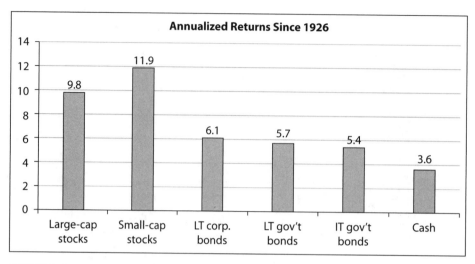

FIGURE 3–2 Historic Performance

Over time, risker assets such as small-company stocks outperform safer investments like cash.

Source: Ibbotson Associates

How You Are Paid

Equities pay investors in two ways: through capital appreciation and through dividends.

Capital Appreciation

Capital appreciation is a fancy term denoting that the price of a stock is likely to rise over time. For instance, in 1986, when the software giant Microsoft went public, its shares were trading at today's equivalent of about 7 cents a share, after factoring in all of the company's stock splits and other adjustments over time. This means that if you had bought today's equivalent of 10,000 shares of Microsoft back then, it would have cost you roughly $700. In 2013, those same 10,000 shares of the world's largest software company would be worth approximately $340,000. In other words, you would have earned approximately 26 percent on your original investment annually for the past 27 years. That's the power of capital appreciation.

Dividends

Price gains aren't the only way stocks can potentially reward you. Most publicly traded companies also return to their shareholders a share of the company's profits through routine **dividend payments**. Think of a dividend as a regular payment that most companies send to shareholders every quarter to entice investors to keep holding onto that company's shares.

From management's perspective, a stable shareholder base—where investors hang on to the firm's stock not just for months but for years—gives the business time to execute its business plan without having to worry about day-to-day volatility caused by disruptions in the company's stock price.

As a result, the majority of companies in the Standard & Poor's 500 index of the largest U.S. stocks pay dividends to their shareholders. Not only that, many of the most successful companies keep their shareholder base steady by not only paying out dividends, but also increasing those payouts year in and year out. Some companies, in fact, such as those found in the Standard & Poor's Dividend Aristocrats Index (whose membership includes ExxonMobil, Johnson & Johnson, McDonald's, and Coca-Cola) have paid and *raised* dividends every year for at least a quarter century.

Dividends are typically paid quarterly. So if a company issues 50 cents in dividends per share per quarter in a given year, you the investor would receive $2 in total payments for every share you owned. Now let's say the stock sells for $50 a share. To calculate your dividend yield, you would take that annual dividend figure and divide it by the share price (Figure 3-3). In other words, divide $2 by $50, resulting in 4 percent. Overall, the average dividend yield for stocks in the S&P 500 index is around 2 percent, so any stock paying 3 percent or higher is considered a high yielder.

$$\text{Dividend Yield} = \frac{\text{Annual Dividends per Share}}{\text{Price per Share}}$$

FIGURE 3–3 Dividend Yield Formula

Total Returns

In this example, let's assume that the stock in question goes from $50 a share to $55 a share over the course of the next 12 months. That would mean that the stock gained 10 percent in value over a year's time. To calculate the so-called **total return** of a stock—in other words, the overall gains you earn by owning shares of a particular company—you would simply add the price gains (in this case 10 percent) to the stock's dividend yield (in this case 4 percent). That would give you a total return of 14 percent, which is better than the 10 percent average long-term total return for equities.

The majority of your gains in this example would have come from price appreciation. So are dividends that important? Yes. For one thing, historically they've accounted for 40 percent of the total return that equities have delivered. But that's the overall long-term average. In some decades, dividends represent a majority of the gains (Figure 3-4). Think back to modest or poor decades for stock price appreciation, such as the 1970s and 1940s. There are also times, like the 2000s, where dividends can account for *all* of your total returns. Indeed, in the so-called lost decade for stocks that ran from 2000 to 2010, the S&P 500 actually lost value over a 10-year span, going from a level of 1,469 to 1,115. So the only positive gains that investors earned during that stretch came from dividends.

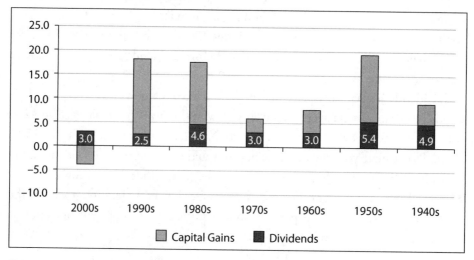

FIGURE 3–4 The Power of Dividends
In many decades, dividends accounted for half of stocks' total returns.
Source: Ibbotson Associates, Hartford

What Are the Potential Risks and Returns?

Key Stats for Large-Company Stocks

Average annual returns: 9.8 percent

Best one-year performance: 54.0 percent in 1933

Worst one-year performance: –43.4 percent in 1931

Number of positive years since 1926: 62

Standard deviation: 20.3

Key Stats for Small-Company Stocks

Average annual returns: 11.9 percent

Best one-year performance: 142.9 percent in 1933

Worst one-year performance: −58.0 percent in 1937

Number of positive years since 1926: 59

Standard deviation: 32.5

At the 30,000-foot level, there are certain key things you need to know about equities. For one thing, even though stocks have historically delivered greater growth to investors over the very long run, in the short run, stocks and bonds and other assets have generally taken turns leading—and lagging—the overall market (Table 3-1). For instance, stocks most recently outpaced bonds in 2012, 2010, and 2009. But they were handily beaten by fixed income in 2011 and, of course, in 2008, when the financial crisis sent stocks tumbling 37 percent while bonds produced modest gains of about 5 percent.

You can't simply rely on the big picture, though, when analyzing stocks, bonds, and other assets. In fact, the risks and returns of stocks depend largely on what types of equities you're talking about.

TABLE 3–1 Taking Turns *In the short run, there's no way to tell which major assets will lead the charge.*	
	Top-Performing Core Asset
2012	Stocks
2011	Bonds
2010	Stocks
2009	Stocks
2008	Bonds
2007	Bonds
2006	Stocks
2005	Bonds
2004	Stocks
2003	Stocks

Source: MFS, Ibbotson

Large Stocks

Often referred to as blue chips, large stocks are shares of companies with a market capitalization—the value that investors collectively ascribe to a company based on the current price of its shares—of $10 billion or higher. Note that market value is not the same as a company's total sales or its so-called book value, which represents all the assets that a business holds on its balance sheet. Market capitalization is simply the market's opinion about what a company is worth at any given moment.

To figure out a company's market cap, you simply take the total number of shares it has outstanding and multiply that by the current share price. Or, simply look to the companies in the S&P 500 index of blue chip stocks.

Examples

Among the biggest large-capitalization companies in the United States are firms such as Apple, ExxonMobil, General Electric, and IBM, all with market capitalizations in excess of $200 billion. You can find large-cap stocks in indexes such as the S&P 500, the Russell 1000 index of blue chip stocks, or the Dow Jones Industrial Average, which represent 30 large companies that the editors of the *Wall Street Journal* deem to be the most reflective of the industrial economy.

The Role Stocks Play in Your Portfolio

Large U.S. stocks are really designed to anchor your portfolio. That's in part because they represent among the most stable parts of the global market. After all, a company worth $100 billion is not likely to go out of business soon. (Of course, the other side of this coin is that the odds of doubling or tripling your money quickly through a blue chip stock aren't that great either, because these companies are known quantities that, by definition, can't fly under the radar.)

Another reason why large stocks should serve as a core part of your investments: the collective market value of large U.S. companies in the S&P 500 index represents around 80 percent of the total value of all domestic stocks. This means that if you own this group of equities, you pretty much own most of the market.

Just as stocks and bonds take turns leading the market, large stocks take turns with other types of equities when it comes to outperforming. Typically, the market goes through a series of changes throughout an economic cycle. And large stocks, which appeal to more conservative-minded investors, tend to do well in the latter phases of an economic recovery (often, at least three years into a rebound), after more aggressive investors have taken fliers with more risky types of equities.

Small Stocks

Why invest in shares of small businesses? Well, when you invest in small-company stocks, you aren't really buying a part of a small business per se. Small-company stocks are defined as shares of firms with market capitalizations of around $2 billion, and by most standards that suggests an established, robust company. They are small only in comparison to large-cap shares.

If large companies provide stability, small-company stocks offer the *potential* for some flash. They offer the potential to grow immensely in scale, something that large-company stocks may not be able to do given the size they've already achieved.

Over time, small-company shares actually deliver slightly higher returns than large-company stocks. According to Ibbotson, the long-term historic annualized return for small stocks is 11.9 percent, versus around 10 percent for blue chip shares. And in their best calendar year, small stocks more than doubled investors' money, which is something that large-cap stocks can't claim. In fact, the best single year for blue chip stocks was about a third as impressive as that of small-company stocks.

The 2000s were the best recent example of why it makes sense to invest in small stocks. At a time when large-cap shares declined in value, small-company stocks posted respectable gains of more than 6 percent annually.

If that's the case, maybe the better question is, why invest in large stocks? As has been noted, the greater the *potential* return, the bigger the *real* risk that an investment poses. In this case, when small stocks lose, they tend to fall much further than their bigger cousins. In their worst 12-month stretch, for example, small stocks shed nearly 60 percent of their value. Compare that to a 43 percent decline for large caps in their worst year. A little extra time doesn't necessarily make things better for small caps. In their worst five-year stretch, small stocks still managed to lose nearly a third of their value, while shares of large companies fell only about 12 percent in their worst five-year performance.

Examples

While small stocks aren't as dominant as blue chips, chances are you've probably heard of many of these types of companies. Among the more widely held small stocks are names such as the home builder Toll Brothers, the website TripAdvisor, the retailer Foot Locker, and the media company Gannett. You can look up the full array of small-company shares in indexes such as the Russell 2000 index and the S&P 600 index of small stocks.

The Role They Play in Your Portfolio

Given the risks that small-cap shares pose, conventional wisdom says that small-company stocks should play a small but core role in your investments. A common way investors make the decision about how much to invest in small stocks is to look at the footprint of small stocks in the broader market.

Overall, based on market, small-company shares represent anywhere from 10 to 20 percent of the overall domestic market's value (Figure 3-5). So that's a good place to start—by placing about 10 to 20 percent of your domestic stocks in these types of companies.

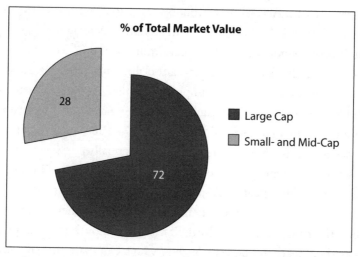

% of Total Market Value

■ Large Cap
▢ Small- and Mid-Cap

FIGURE 3–5 Breakdown of U.S. Stock Market
Large-cap stocks make up the vast majority of the market's value.

Source: Morningstar

Growth Stocks

While equities in general are known for their potential for growth, not all equities are considered growth stocks. Investors divide the universe of stocks in many ways, and one key distinction is between growth- and value-oriented shares.

What's the difference? In general, growth stocks tend to be shares of companies whose profits are expanding at a faster rate than the overall market. This is important because over long periods of time, there's a relationship between a company's earnings growth rate and the rate of returns generated by its shares. In the short run, this relationship may not necessarily manifest itself. For instance, a company's stock could easily rise in value in a year in which the firm loses money; similarly, a stock's price could fall at a time when the underlying company posts strong profits.

To really understand what growth stocks are, it's useful to think about a car analogy. Growth-oriented shares are like high-performance vehicles that tend to go really fast. Well, you know that if you want to buy a high-performance sports car that goes faster than a normal vehicle, you'll have to pay up.

And that's the case with growth stocks. In exchange for the speed with which these companies are growing, investors are often willing to pay higher prices for these stocks. In this case, those prices are reflected in something called a **price/ earnings (P/E) ratio.**

Every stock has a P/E ratio. This figure is calculated by taking a stock's current share price and dividing it by the underlying company's annual earnings per share. For example, if a stock is trading at $75 a share while the company posts annual earnings of $5 a share, its P/E ratio would be 15. Historically, the broad market's average ratio has stood at around 16, so any stock trading above that level has a good chance of being considered growth.

Examples

Historically, growth stocks tend to be found in certain sectors of the economy, such as technology. Throughout the 1990s, for example, tech giants like Microsoft, Intel, and Cisco Systems were deemed classic growth shares. Other traditional sectors that are growth oriented include healthcare and consumer discretionary companies, which make consumer goods that people want (like cars) as opposed to need (like household goods) (Table 3-2).

But over time, companies and even sectors can shift from value to growth and vice versa. In fact, Microsoft, Intel, and Cisco are all in some circles considered value stocks (we'll get to those in a second) because their profits are all growing in line with or slower than the broad market; their shares are cheaper than the market as a whole; and they're purchased just as much for the dividends they offer as for their potential for capital gains.

TABLE 3–2 S&P 500 Growth Sectors
While not all stocks in these sectors are "growth" shares, most are.
Growth
Technology
Healthcare
Consumer discretionary
Industrials
Basic materials

Source: Morningstar

This doesn't mean that technology is no longer a growth sector. Today, faster-growing companies in this industry are now the standard-bearers of growth. They include names such as Google, Apple, and Amazon.com.

The Role They Play in Your Portfolio

Like small stocks, growth-oriented stocks can, at times, provide a bit of a punch to your portfolio, especially in the early phases of an economic rebound. For example, in 2009, in the first year of the post–Great Recession recovery, growth stocks gained more than 30 percent while value advanced a more modest 20 percent.

Growth and value shares, however, take turns leading the market. Growth, for instance, was in fashion throughout the 1990s bull market. Value, on the other hand, outperformed starting in 2000. More recently, while growth beat value in the recovery year of 2009, value lost less than growth did in 2008, when the stock market crashed.

In either case, the idea is to balance your portfolio with both growth and value. If you own a broad-based S&P 500 index fund—a passively managed portfolio that simply mimics the S&P 500—then half of your position is already in growth.

Value Stocks

If growth stocks are like sports cars that you pay top dollar for, value-oriented shares are like junkers that you buy for pennies on the dollar. By definition, value stocks are shares of companies that investors undervalue because they're overlooked or beaten down.

In some cases, a company is undervalued through no fault of its own; its shares may simply be ignored because other, more appealing opportunities may present themselves to investors. In other cases, a value stock is beaten down because the company made missteps or bad decisions that led to poor performance. In either case, whether the car is dinged up because of the fault of the driver, or if it's simply overlooked because it's not as attractive as a Ferrari, value shares sell for discounted prices in the bargain lot.

Indeed, the average price/earnings ratio for value stocks stood at around 12 in 2013, whereas the typical P/E ratio for growth shares was more than 17.

Besides a lower-than-average P/E, value stocks are marked by other characteristics. For starters, value shares tend to pay higher dividends than growth stocks. The average dividend yield for large-cap value shares, for instance, recently stood at 2.6 percent. By comparison, the typical yield for the overall market recently stood at 2 percent, while the yield for large-cap growth shares was recently 1.8 percent.

This is typically the case because companies whose shares are classified as value tend to grow more slowly than growth stocks. The average annual long-term earnings growth rate for growth stocks, for instance, was recently 11 percent, while profits for value-oriented companies were recently expanding at an annual rate of around 8 percent. So to compete for investor interest, value stocks have to pay more in income to entice investors to stick around.

Examples

Value stocks also tend to be concentrated in certain sectors of the economy, many of which are deemed to be defensive, such as utilities, consumer staples, and financials (Table 3-3). Among the biggest stocks in the United States, classic value stocks include General Electric, ExxonMobil, Walmart, and J.P. Morgan Chase.

TABLE 3–3 S&P 500 Value Sectors *While not all stocks in these sectors are "value" shares, most are.*
Value
Utilities
Energy
Consumer Staples
Financials
Telecommunications

Source: Morningstar

The Role They Play in Your Portfolio

Value stocks pose somewhat of a conundrum. While value-oriented companies tend to generate slower profit growth, they actually have a long history of performing better over time than growth companies. Why? Part of it could be because value investors exploit mispricing in the market. Even if you believe that the stock market is totally rational, you probably accept the fact that from time to time, investors misjudge the true value of a company. When they overvalue the prospects for growth stocks, that tends to weigh down the prices of those shares. But when it comes to value stocks, investors often err by overly punishing or overlooking companies that have made mistakes.

Also, value is the essence of contrarianism. It goes to the heart of that famous Warren Buffett saying, "Be greedy when others are fearful and fearful when others are greedy." Plus, as the tech crash of 2000 and the housing crash of 2008 demonstrated, the price investors pay for assets is critical. Over time, in a rational market, investors will eventually adjust the price of an investment to accurately reflect its intrinsic value. If said investment starts off being overpriced, that could in theory weigh down the shares for years. On the other hand, an undervalued stock is very likely to rise to fully reflect a company's rightful worth.

This is why conventional wisdom says that at the very least, investors ought to divide their domestic holdings down the middle, with 50 percent in growth and 50 percent in value. But there's also another school of thought that states that because of the long-standing premium that investors ascribe to value shares—and because of their higher dividend payments (which represent a bird in the hand, even if it's not two in the bush)—you ought to tilt your portfolio slightly more toward value. We will discuss just how to do that later on in this book.

Foreign Stocks

It used to be that shares of companies domiciled overseas were considered exotic by individual investors. Not anymore. Thanks to globalization, which has spread commerce to all corners of the planet, you're probably just as likely to have heard of foreign companies—and to buy their goods and services—as you are to be a customer of an American-based firm. For just as U.S. companies like Apple have a global footprint (some of their products are designed in the United States, made in China, but sold throughout the world), so too do blue chip foreign companies.

Unilever, for instance, may be headquartered in Switzerland, but you're more than familiar with its brand names, such as Dove soap, Lipton tea, and Breyer's ice cream.

Diageo is a spirits company based in the United Kingdom, but you've no doubt heard of its Guinness beers, its Johnnie Walker whiskies, and its Ketel One vodkas.

There are a few key reasons why you want to own foreign stocks. For starters, companies headquartered in the United States and listed on U.S. exchanges represent less than half of the total stock market capitalization of the world. So if you were to forgo investing abroad, you would be missing an opportunity set of shares that's bigger than the entire U.S. stock market. Among this group are companies that are just as successful and potentially just as rewarding as U.S. stocks. This ranges from technology companies (such as China's Baidu and South Korea's Samsung) to healthcare firms (such as Swiss-based Novartis) to manufacturers (such as Japan's Toyota and Honda) to financials (such as the U.K.'s HSBC and Barclays) to retailers (such as Sweden's Ikea and Spain's Inditex, which owns the Zara chain).

Moreover, there's the diversification aspect to consider. Even with globalization, the economies of the United States, Western Europe, Eastern Europe, China, Latin America, and Africa all work in slightly different cycles. When one is in recession, another may simply be in a slowdown, while other parts of the world may be booming economically. As a result, there is still some diversification in owning foreign stocks, even if that benefit has fallen a bit in recent years (Figure 3-6).

What's more, even if there is very little diversification benefit from owning foreign stocks—if U.S. and overseas shares move in the same direction all the

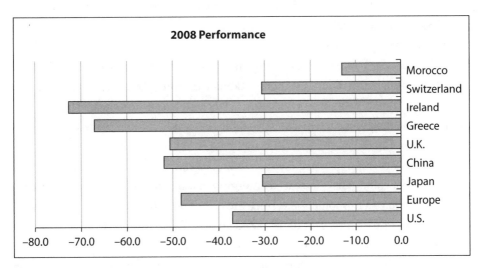

FIGURE 3–6 Foreign Diversification
Though foreign markets all lost ground in 2008, they fell by varying amounts.

Source: MSCI

time—international equities will not necessarily produce the exact same results. In other words, when the U.S. market zigs, foreign stocks will likely also zig (instead of zagging), but they may not zig to the same degree. Case in point: In 2008, when the global financial crisis sent stocks in almost every country sinking, the United States lost 37 percent. That same year, Japanese and Swiss stocks lost less than the United States; they were down about 30 percent. On the other hand, the United Kingdom and Italy lost more; they fell more than 50 percent.

The same phenomenon took place the following year, when virtually every global stock market rose in lockstep as the financial panic wore off. In 2009, American stocks rose 26 percent in value. In that same year, foreign stocks moved in the same direction, but Canadian and Swedish stocks climbed more than 50 percent, while Japanese and Irish stocks gained less than 10 percent.

The lesson here is that even though there wasn't a technical diversification benefit by going global (since all these markets moved in lockstep), the variability of returns around the world were sufficient reason to want to spread your bets internationally to ensure that all your money isn't tied to the one stock market that happens to be performing the worst in any particular time period.

Distinctions

Within the world of foreign equities, there's one key distinction to make. Shares of companies headquartered in the mature economies of Western Europe, Japan, Hong Kong, Canada, Australia, and New Zealand are generally referred to as **developed market foreign stocks**.

Again, developed market blue chip stocks are shares of firms you've most likely heard of, such as Unilever, Nestlé, Toyota, Honda, HSBC, and Diageo. Because they are domiciled in older and more established economies, these shares tend to behave in a similar fashion to U.S. equities (though this is not always the case). In other words, they tend to be relatively stable.

By comparison, shares of firms that are based in newer and faster-growing economies in the developing world—which includes large swaths of Latin America, Eastern Europe, and Asia—are called **emerging market stocks**. Now, the term *emerging* can be a bit of a misnomer here, since the emerging market classification includes some of the world's largest economies based on overall activity and trade. These countries include China, India, South Korea, and Brazil. China and India, in fact, happen to be two of the five largest economies in the world, with China on track to soon eclipse the United States as the biggest economic force on the planet.

Also within those countries, there are companies that, while classified as emerging market stocks, are just as known for being blue chip global leaders as their developed market counterparts. Samsung, for instance, which is Apple's biggest competitor in the smartphone space, is headquartered in South Korea. PetroChina, based in China, has overtaken ExxonMobil as the world's largest oil company.

Emerging market stocks can provide some added zip to your potential returns—over the past 15 years, which were a depressed period for global stocks, emerging market equities gained around 10 percent annually, versus around 4 percent for developed market shares. (This disparity is partly because emerging market economies are growing so much faster than the developed world. While the U.S. economy has recently been expanding at less than 3 percent a year, and while much of Europe has been growing even more slowly, the emerging world economies have been expanding at closer to 6 percent annually.)

At the same time, though, emerging market equities can expose you to additional risks. Emerging market stocks, for instance, tend to be much more volatile than developed market shares, meaning that in good years they can climb faster, but in bad years they can fall further. In 2008, for example, a typical emerging market stock lost more than half its value, whereas developed market stocks fell about 40 percent (Table 3-4).

TABLE 3–4 Emerging Markets Versus Developed Markets *Emerging market stocks tend to experience higher highs and lower lows.*		
	Emerging Market Stocks	**Developed Market Stocks**
2012	18.5	17.3
2011	−21.6	12.1
2010	21.6	7.8
2009	62.1	31.8
2008	−48.5	−43.4
2007	39.5	11.2
2006	29.5	26.3
2005	33.1	13.5
2004	27.6	20.3
2003	56.0	38.6

Source: Morningstar

Why the added risk? Simple. For starters, because the emerging world is made up of younger economies, companies based there—even large, established ones—tend to be younger themselves and less fully developed than their counterparts in Europe and Japan.

Moreover, there are *political risks* that emerging market companies encounter that Western Europe and Japan are unlikely to face. Even though many emerging market firms sell globally, the fact that they are domiciled in relatively unstable economies can affect the value that global investors assign to them. Political problems that crop up in the emerging world—like recent coups in Thailand and Egypt—will surely have an impact on any organization based in those places.

Another offshoot of political risk is *currency risk*. Even modest changes to the value of a local economy's currency can have a big impact on a company's ability to sell its goods at prices that are competitive with global peers. What's more, currency shifts can have a huge impact on the cost of sourcing raw materials that go into producing those products. You probably recall that in the late 1990s, the emerging world was wracked by a currency crisis referred to as the "Asian Flu" that began with the collapse of the Thai baht but that quickly spread like an epidemic to South Korea, Indonesia, the Philippines, Malaysia, and other parts of Asia. In fact, it eventually spread to Eastern Europe and Russia, and it was one of the reasons the Russian government was forced to default on its debt in 1998.

The developed world must also contend with fluctuations in currency values. But because the euro and the dollar are currencies of record—for instance, much of global commerce, including the buying and selling of commodities, is conducted in those currencies—the swings tend to be more orderly and modest. This gives foreign companies in the developed world an additional advantage of stability and relative safety.

The Role They Play in Your Portfolio

Both foreign developed market stocks and emerging market shares deserve a permanent place in a well-diversified stock portfolio. The question is, how big a role should they play? In the past, conventional wisdom said that you need to keep only a small portion of your money overseas, perhaps as little as 10 percent. Then more recently, a new school of thought emerged that said that investors should allocate their foreign equities based on the percentage of the world's total market capitalization that international stocks represent. That would mean putting 60 percent or more of your stock portfolio in foreign companies. But there are risks to being so bold with foreign shares, especially since that would mean that the vast majority of your investments would be sourced in foreign currencies, even though you'll end up paying for your food, basic needs, and eventually your retirement in U.S. dollars.

In most cases, you'll find that the answer for how much you should keep overseas probably lies somewhere in between these extremes. In fact, a recent study by the Vanguard Group, the giant mutual fund manager, showed that you can target a 40 percent allocation of your overall stock portfolio to foreign shares (this would be a combination of your developed and emerging market stakes). At 40 percent, you would get the full effects of diversification, Vanguard found. Past that level, as we'll discuss in later chapters, additional foreign holdings cease making your portfolio more stable and will actually increase the volatility of your strategy.

As for emerging market stocks, given their high-risk but high-return characteristics, you probably want a good slug of them as part of your overall international stock stake. But you would not want to keep the majority of your foreign holdings in the emerging world, given the amount of volatility that could add to your portfolio. Here, too, it's useful to think about 40 percent as a target. In other words, an emerging market stake that's about a third to 40 percent of your overall foreign holdings is a good place to start.

Your Bonds

The second major asset category is bonds.

What They Are

When you buy a stock, you're a part owner of a business. When you buy a bond, on the other hand, you are a *banker* to that business—or government, or government-related agency that requires debt financing. You're the lender, and the bond is the IOU.

This arrangement, while legally complicated, is really quite simple. When you buy a bond, you agree to loan the bond issuer a certain amount of money in exchange for a certain amount of interest to be paid at routine intervals over a set number of years as stipulated in the bond contract. In addition, the bond's maturity date stipulates what the life of the loan will be and when the bond issuer agrees to return the principal loan amount to you at an agreed-upon date.

This means that there's a lot of certainty built into this type of investment. You know, for instance, exactly how much money you'll make in interest over the course of the loan and when you'll get your money back. True, there is one big uncertainty lurking out there—and that's the chance, slim as it may be, that a government or corporation that you lend money to will be short or late with its promised interest payments or will ultimately default on the loan itself. But you can build in some safeguards. For instance, the greater the chance that a bond issuer might default (for instance, if it has a poor credit rating by the major agencies, or if it has a history of defaults or near defaults), the higher the interest rate that investors will demand to buy those bonds.

All of this certainty may sound appealing, but it limits the amount of money you can expect to earn on this type of investment. For it stands to reason that if high risk is associated with high return, then high certainty (or low risk) must be linked to smaller potential gains. That's certainly been the case over the past century. Since 1926, the average bond has returned around 6 percent a year, which is significantly less than the returns for equities.

You can understand why. Being a banker really restricts what you can expect to earn on this type of investment. Shares of a stock can theoretically grow without limit, based on the successful expansion of the underlying business. But if you lend money to a business, it matters little whether the company is a growing or stagnant concern, whether it's a mom-and-pop operation or Walmart. All that really matters is whether the business is successful *enough* to pay you your interest on time and return your principal loan amount at the agreed-upon date.

Why You Need Them

The obvious question is, if stocks earn you more money, why invest in bonds at all?

Ballast

Well, the downside of owning high-returning stocks, of course, is that they come with a high degree of volatility. Bonds, because of their more stable and staid nature, can help reduce that rockiness in your portfolio by delivering more predictable and muted returns.

Indeed, bonds may not make you nearly the amount that stocks do, but historically, they've posted positive returns more frequently than equities. For instance, since 1926, intermediate-term government bonds (those maturing in around five years or so) have made investors money in 77 calendar years, versus 62 for large-cap stocks and just 59 for small-company equities. Not only that, but in the few years in which bonds have lost money, they lost significantly less than did equities.

The worst 12-month stretch on record for intermediate-term government bonds, for instance, was an average drop of about 5 percent in 1994. Compare that to the 43 percent loss for large stocks in 1931 and a 58 percent decline for small stocks in 1937 (Table 3-5). In other words, in the worst calendar year for bonds, $100,000 would have turned into $95,000. Yet in the worst-case scenario for equities, your $100,000 would have shrunk to $57,000 or $42,000, respectively. That's a huge difference.

TABLE 3–5 Worst Losses in Stocks and Bonds *Bonds tend to lose far less than stocks in a worst-case scenario.*		
	Stocks	**Bonds**
1-Year Periods	–43.3%	–5.1%
5-year Periods	–12.5%	1.0%
10-Year Periods	–1.4%	1.3%
20-Year Periods	3.1%	1.6%

Source: Ibbotson Associates

Adding even a modest amount of bonds to your stock portfolio can significantly reduce the types of losses you can expect in a major downturn or correction (Table 3-6). In the financial crisis in 2008, for example, a 100 percent stock portfolio sank 37 percent. Had you shifted a mere 30 percent of your money out of stocks and into bonds before that year, that loss would have been reduced to 24 percent. And in the worst year for stocks, a 30 percent slug in bonds would have reduced your losses of 43 percent to 32 percent.

Diversification

While it's true that stocks outperform bonds in the long run, there are plenty of occasions when bonds outpace equities in the short term—in some cases for one or two years, in others for nearly a decade (Table 3-7). In the so-called lost decade for stocks between 2000 and 2010, when the S&P 500 index actually declined (a rarity for equities), blue chip shares posted losses of nearly 1 percent a year. Yet during that same stretch, long-term government bonds (which invest in government debt maturing in around 20 years) gained an impressive 8 percent a year in total returns, while intermediate-term government bonds returned more than 6 percent.

TABLE 3–6 Worst Losses by Stock and Bond Allocation
Adding bonds to your portfolio will help lessen the fall in a crisis.

Allocation	Worst 1-Yr	Worst 5-Yr	Worst 10-Yr	Worst 20-Yr
100% Stocks	–43.3%	–12.5%	–1.4%	3.1%
90% Stocks/ 10% Bonds	–39.7%	–10.3%	–0.3%	3.6%
70% Stocks/ 30% Bonds	–32.3%	–6.3%	1.7%	4.3%
50% Stocks/ 50% Bonds	–24.7%	–2.8%	2.0%	4.6%
30% Stocks/ 70% Bonds	–17.0%	0.1%	2.1%	3.6%
10% Stocks/ 90% Bonds	–11.2%	–1.4%	1.8%	2.0%

Source: Ibbotson Associates

TABLE 3–7 Stocks Versus Bonds by Decade
Annualized total returns for equities and fixed-income investments by decade.

	Stocks	Bonds
2000s	–0.9%	7.7%
1990s	18.2%	8.8%
1980s	17.6%	12.6%
1970s	5.9%	5.5%
1960s	7.8%	1.4%
1950s	19.4%	–0.1%
1940s	9.2%	3.2%
1930s	–0.1%	4.9%
1920s	19.2%	5.0%

Source: Ibbotson Associates

The point is, it is impossible to predict with certainty when bonds will take a backseat to equities and when they won't. But here's what we do know: The two asset classes directly compete for investor dollars, so when investors sour on the prospects for one, it's more than likely that they will turn to the other to make a profit.

A classic example was during the bursting of the technology stock bubble in early 2000. Once the market's mania for Internet stocks died down at the end of 1999 and investors realized that the stock market was more expensive than it had been in decades, equities posted three consecutive years of losses. The S&P 500 fell 9 percent in 2000, 12 percent in 2001, and more than 22 percent in 2002. In that same stretch, intermediate-term government bonds gained nearly 13 percent in 2000, nearly 8 percent in 2001, and nearly 13 percent in 2002.

Income

Not all investors care about whether bonds are set to outperform stocks, or whether bonds can help dampen the volatility of their overall portfolio. For many investors, especially retired ones, the most appealing attribute of bonds is the income that they produce.

Like stocks, bonds make you money in a couple of ways. Here, the biggest component of returns comes from the coupon on the bond, or the interest that it pays you until maturity. But unlike stock dividends, which companies routinely increase on an annual basis to help keep pace with inflation, bond interest is fixed. Hence, bonds are often referred to as fixed-income investments.

In recent years, bond yields have fallen to historic lows, but even at these levels, the fixed interest that bonds pay is still among the best sources of income. Consider that the average dividend yield for stocks in the S&P 500 index of blue chip stocks was recently just 2 percent. A typical bank certificate of deposit was paying less than 1 percent in 2013. The average savings account was yielding less than half a percentage point. And the yield on the typical money market mutual fund was less than a tenth of one percent. Against this backdrop, even the paltry 3 percent yield on a 10-year Treasury bond may have some appeal for income-minded investors.

Of course, interest is not the only way that fixed-income investments pay you. Like stocks, bonds once issued can trade on the open market. So the total return you earn from your bonds or bond funds represents the combination of the yield you earn plus whatever price gain (or loss) there is on the security itself.

Why would a bond's value fluctuate in the open market? Well, if financial problems beset the bond issuer, whether it's a company or a government, investors are likely to fear the potential for a possible default. In that case, they'd be likely to sell some of their bonds to other investors who are willing to assume that risk in exchange for taking a haircut on the price of the underlying investment. Just look back to the European debt crisis. When it started to appear as if financially strapped governments in Greece, Italy, Spain, and Portugal might not be able to meet all of their obligations, investors began selling their bonds, driving down prices. Conversely, if the finances of a company or government that was considered a default risk were to improve—or, say, if the underlying economy improves, removing a threat to a vulnerable bond issuer—then investors might gravitate toward those investments, driving up the price.

Another possibility has to do with interest rates. One of the key things you need to understand is that the price of fixed-income investments is inversely related to market interest rates. If rates were to fall, as they did for a 30-year stretch starting in the early 1980s, then the price of new bonds would rise.

If you stop and think about it, this makes perfect sense. Let's assume that market rates were at, say, 5 percent when the U.S. Treasury issued a batch of bonds. Then assume that over the next year or two, those rates gradually fall to 4 percent, meaning that new Treasury securities would come with a 4 percent coupon. Well, if you happen to own the older 5 percent bonds, you'd likely see tremendous demand for those older and higher-yielding bonds. And with greater demand, the underlying bond price would rise. Conversely, if market rates were to rise—which is greatly expected after a three-decade decline—the bond prices would likely fall, since in that case, newer bonds would start yielding more than older ones, driving down their demand and prices.

What Are the Potential Risks and Returns?

Key Stats for Bonds

Average annual returns: 5.7 percent

Best one-year performance: 40.4 percent in 1982

Worst one-year performance: –14.9 percent in 2009

Number of positive years since 1926: 64

Standard deviation: 9.8

Key Stats for High-Quality Corporate Bonds

Average annual returns: 6.1 percent

Best one-year performance: 42.6 percent in 1982

Worst one-year performance: –8.1 percent in 1969

Number of positive years since 1926: 69

Standard deviation: 8.4

While bonds are relatively safer than stocks, they are not risk free. Indeed, it is important to be aware of two major risks that bonds expose investors to. The first is called **credit risk**.

Anytime you lend a government or company money, there is a slight possibility that the borrower will not be able to pay you the interest that was originally promised. Moreover, there's the risk that you may not even get the principal amount of the loan back when the loan matures. While defaults like this are rare among government and corporate debt, they're not unheard of.

In the late 1990s, for instance, the Russian government was forced to default on some of its obligations due to economic troubles caused by a regional currency crisis. In 2002, Argentina and other Latin American countries followed suit under the crush of mounting debt. More recently, Greece and other European nations teetered on the brink of default caused by their fiscal crisis and a regionwide recession. Defaults aren't limited to governments. Amid the global financial panic, a number of corporations ran into financial problems and were forced to file for bankruptcy. Among them was the auto giant General Motors.

The rule of thumb is, the greater the likelihood that a bond issuer will default, the more that borrower has to pay you in interest for compensation. This is why bonds issued by corporations with poor credit ratings—sometimes called junk or non-investment-grade bonds—pay considerably higher interest to their investors than those issued by fiscally sound, high-quality companies. Meanwhile, government bonds issued by the United States tend to pay the lowest interest because of the perceived strength of the U.S. Treasury.

The other major risk that bonds expose you from is called **interest rate risk**. This is the possibility that market interest rates will rise over time, making older, lower-yielding investments less attractive. Bonds owners faced very low interest rates over the past three decades, as interest rates have fallen for an entire generation. In fact, since peaking in 1982, the yield on the 10-year Treasury bond has collapsed from a high of nearly 16 percent in 1981 to as low as around 1.6 percent 31 years later (Figure 3-7).

Because rates move in the opposite direction from bond prices, fixed-income investments enjoyed the tailwind of rising prices amid falling yields. Moving forward, many market observers fear that as bond yields rebound as the global economy heals, it's likely that bond prices will be weighed down by rising rates. And that could reduce the returns that bonds might provide while increasing the interest rate risk that they expose you to.

As with stocks, though, the risk and return profile of a bond depends on what type of bond you're talking about:

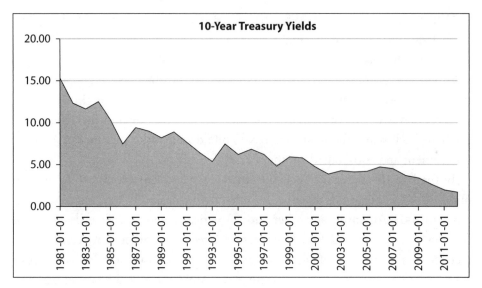

FIGURE 3–7 Bond Yields over Time
Yields on 10-Year Treasuries have been falling precipitously.

Data shown is from September 1 of each year. *Source:* St. Louis Fed

U.S. Government Debt

Among domestic bonds, the most widely available are government-issued securities. And the most common forms of government debt are U.S. Treasury bills, notes, and bonds. This isn't that surprising. With stocks, the biggest companies based on market value hold the most sway over the markets. This is why successful businesses like Apple, ExxonMobil, and General Electric are the biggest companies in the U.S. stock market.

When it comes to the bond market, though, the biggest debtors hold the most sway. And few governments owe as much in total as the United States.

However, U.S. Treasury debt is considered among the safest when it comes to credit risk. That's because Treasuries are backed by the full faith and credit of the U.S. government. Theoretically, if Uncle Sam were in a bind and could not afford to pay back his obligations, the Treasury could always resort to printing more dollars to make good on the government's debts.

This is a power that no company and few governments really have. This is why, despite the fact that many investors question the fiscal health of Washington, D.C., they have not abandoned Treasuries, and these bonds pay among the lowest yields on the planet (Figure 3-8).

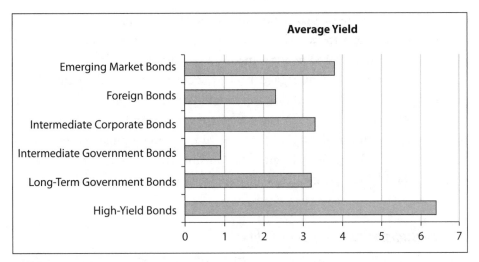

FIGURE 3–8 Yield by Bond Type
Varying yields on different types of bonds is another reason to diversify.

Source: Morningstar

Treasury bonds are not riskless, however. More than any other bond, this form of debt is vulnerable to interest rate risk. This would explain why long-term government bonds (those that mature in around 20 years) have lost value more frequently than corporate bonds have—22 years since 1926. Moreover, if rates were to really spike, the losses could be noticeable. The worst one-year loss for long-term Treasuries was a decline of nearly 15 percent in 2009.

High-Quality Corporate Bonds

This is debt issued by companies that earn high marks for safety from the major credit-rating agencies such as Standard & Poor's and Moody's. Investment-grade bonds, which are issued by companies that score between a BBB and an AAA credit rating, expose you to a combination of both credit and interest rate risk.

But because of the strength of the balance sheets of many of these firms, high-quality corporates often have to pay only slightly more than Treasuries do. For example, in 2013, the average yield for a high-grade corporate bond was around 3.3 percent. That was just slightly higher than the 2.6 percent yield on 10-year Treasury bonds. Part of this was because in the aftermath of the financial crisis, many corporations dramatically improved their balance sheets by raising cash and cutting spending.

This does not mean that corporate bonds are devoid of major risks. Like government debt, their prices can be negatively affected by rising market interest rates. And even highly rated bonds sometimes go sour.

Remember that some mortgage-backed securities that led to the global financial panic in 2008 were at one point rated AAA by the major credit-rating agencies. This combination of risks is why corporate bonds have slightly outperformed government debt over the long run, posting annualized returns of 6.1 percent. And this is also why any fixed-income strategy ought to have some corporate bonds to help the fixed-income portion of your portfolio outpace inflation.

Non-Investment-Grade Corporate Debt

Like high-quality corporate bonds, non-investment-grade debt represents loans that you extend to private-sector companies. The only difference is that these bonds happen to be issued by businesses with less-than-pristine balance sheets. For example, these firms may have more debt on their books than financial analysts believe is safe, especially if the economy were to turn south. Some of these firms may also have a history of default or bankruptcy, which leads investors to be wary of them.

As a result, so-called junk bonds expose you to considerably more credit risk than high-quality debt, and therefore they must pay out higher interest rates to attract potential investors. In 2013, the average high-yield bond was paying 6.7 percent, or roughly double what high-quality bonds were forced to pay.

Now, the risks of owning junk bonds aren't as dire as you may think. Historically, the default rate on junk bonds is only around 5 percent, and more recently, that figure has dropped to less than 3 percent. Plus, the higher yield on a junk bond means that it is less vulnerable to the risk of rising market rates. That's because rates would have to really skyrocket before they compete with what older junk bonds are paying.

That said, junk bonds ought to make up a small portion of your portfolio—really, no more than 10 percent—because they do represent the biggest credit risk to your fixed-income portfolio. Moreover, they add a near-stock-like volatility to your mix. In fact, junk bonds are about a third more volatile than high-quality corporate debt and more than twice as risky as Treasuries. In other words, non-investment-grade bonds may offer attractive income, but little safety and no ballast.

Municipal Bonds

These bonds are issued by cities, counties, and states to fund general operations or to build specific projects such as roads, bridges, and public works. While these are technically *government* bonds, towns and states do not have the power to print money as the Treasury does. Therefore, they do expose you to credit risk.

This is why it's important to consider the credit rating of a muni issuer, just as you would with corporate bonds. While some local and state governments are fiscally sound, there are others—like the city of Detroit in 2013—that have been in or are teetering on the brink of bankruptcy.

That said, cities, counties, and states often have the power to tax. Moreover, because the interest on a municipal bond is often federal income tax free (and in many cases, state income tax free too if you are an in-state resident buying an in-state bond), the after-tax income that these bonds throw off can be significantly higher than that of Treasuries.

Foreign Bonds

As with stocks, the bond market has become increasingly global, and it is increasingly easy to purchase the debt of internationally based companies, foreign governments in the developed world, and foreign governments in the emerging world.

While foreign governments aren't considered as safe a credit risk as the United States, many around the world are actually in surprisingly good fiscal health. To be sure, recent fiscal problems among European nations like Greece, Italy, and Spain have raised some fears. But in Europe, Germany is considered as strong a fiscal entity as the United States is regarded in the Americas. Plus, many countries in the emerging world are actually net lenders now, not net borrowers.

Yet because of their relative size and political concerns, governments and corporations based overseas must pay significantly higher yields than the United States. Indeed, the average emerging market corporate was recently paying 5.5 percent (nearly double what U.S. corporate debt was paying), and the typical emerging market government bond was at 5.2 percent. That's double the recent yield on the 10-year Treasury.

Despite the attractiveness of those yields, you do have to be careful with foreign bonds and limit your allocation to them. That's because international bonds expose you to foreign currencies. And often, the currency risk is more of a threat than the underlying credit or interest-rate risk.

QUIZ

1. Stocks are needed because they are the only major asset class that provides ...
   A. Capital appreciation.
   B. Income.
   C. Real growth.

2. Bonds are necessary because they are the only major asset class that provides income.
   A. True
   B. False

3. Stocks are risk-based investments and bonds are riskless investments.
   A. True
   B. False

4. Large and small stocks are distinguishable based on ...
   A. Their profit potential.
   B. Their market value.
   C. Their potential for capital appreciation.

5. Small stocks offer the potential for higher returns. Therefore, small stocks are ...
   A. More risky than other types of stocks.
   B. Less risky than other types of stocks.
   C. Just as risky as other types of stocks.

6. Growth stocks have a tendency to ...
   A. Make you more money than value stocks.
   B. Be more attractive than value stocks.
   C. Be more expensive than the broader market.

7. Small stocks represent about 10 to 20 percent of the total market value of domestic equities. They should represent ...
   A. 10 to 20 percent of your domestic stocks.
   B. Less than 10 to 20 percent of your domestic stocks.
   C. More than 10 to 20 percent of your domestic stocks.

8. **Foreign stocks represent more than half of the total market value of the world's equities. They should represent ...**
    A. Less than half of your stock portfolio.
    B. About half of your stock portfolio.
    C. More than half of your stock portfolio.

9. **Bonds provide your portfolio with ...**
    A. Ballast.
    B. Diversification.
    C. Income.
    D. All of the above.
    E. None of the above.

10. **Corporate bonds return more than government bonds over the long run because ...**
    A. They currently yield more than government bonds.
    B. They currently yield less than government bonds.
    C. They expose investors to more risk than do government bonds.
    D. They expose investors to less risk than do government bonds.

chapter 4

Establishing a Strategic Plan

In establishing a strategic investment plan, you must first consider the factors that determine your basic allocation.

Your Age

Just as with anything in life, there is a cycle to your asset allocation strategy—only this one might seem a tad contrarian. For instance, some may assume that because a 20-something has decades of time in which to build his or her nest egg, he or she can afford to take a slow-and-steady approach that is dominated by conservative investments such as fixed income that grow much slower than stocks.

By contrast, one might assume that an older worker who is just 5 or 10 years away from retirement but who is falling short of reaching his or her goals may want to boost exposure to equities to get to the finish line faster.

This is precisely opposite to the approach you need to take. Academic research and history indicate that the optimal approach is to start aggressively—with the vast majority of your portfolio in equities—and then to gradually grow more conservative over time by adding to your fixed-income stake.

Why? Because time is both friend and enemy to the long-term investor. When you're young, you have ample time to take risks with stocks, since any misfortune that might befall your portfolio early on (such as the bear markets that occurred in 2000–2002 and 2007–2009) can be corrected once the market eventually recovers. Plus, while you're still working—especially if you're young and have expectations for higher earning power later on—you can always make up for market losses in the short run by boosting your savings rate over the long run, made possible in part by your gradually rising salary.

An older worker who is at or near retirement cannot do that, because (a) the market recovery may not happen fast enough to beat that potential retirement date; and (b) there's little time left to be able to boost your savings sufficiently to make up for those losses.

Time, meanwhile, can simultaneously work against you because it allows the deleterious effects of inflation to compound for decades, eating into the potential purchasing power of the portfolio you're investing in. And when you're young, the thought of allowing inflation to eat away at your funds for 40 or more years of work—and potentially another 25 years of retirement—can be scary.

This is why target date mutual funds, which are professionally managed all-in-one asset allocation portfolios, generally start off very aggressive. For young people in their 20s, for instance, the Vanguard Target Retirement 2060 fund and the T. Rowe Price Retirement 2055 fund both maintain about 90 percent exposure to stocks (the numbers in the fund names, by the way, refer to the year in which people assume they will retire).

Over time, though, these target date funds gradually and automatically grow more conservative (in other words, they reduce their exposure to equities) to satisfy the needs of older workers as they age. In fact, for those who are already retired, the Vanguard Target Retirement 2010 fund keeps only 40 percent of its assets in equities. The Fidelity Freedom 2005 target date fund, for those who are well into retirement, maintains only 30 percent exposure to equities.

Your Time Horizon

Your age is not the only factor that goes into figuring out your "time horizon," which is an important determinant of how much risk you can take with stocks.

To truly determine how much exposure you ought to have to equities, you must first figure out when you actually plan to retire. Most asset allocation models that you'll find at financial websites tend to assume a traditional retirement age of 65. In reality, not all workers who plan to work until 65 actually get there. In fact, studies by the Employee Benefit Research Institute show that many workers leave the workforce as many as five years before they planned to because they were laid off and could not find new work or because health reasons prevented them from reaching their goals (Figure 4-1).

	65	66 to 69	70 and Older
Workers' Expectation	25%	10%	26%
Actual Age at Retirement	11%	8%	6%

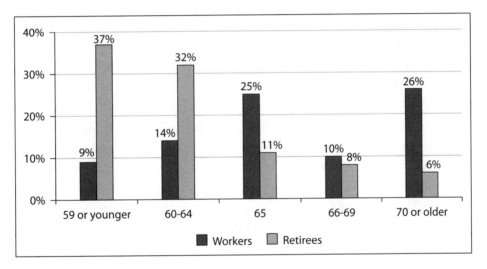

FIGURE 4–1 Retirement Reality
Percent of workers who expect to retire at various ages—and the percent of retirees who retired at those ages.

Source: EBRI

There's another reality: Not all workers want to work until age 65. Some may have distinct plans to retire early, say at 55 or 59. On the other hand, there are those who want and plan to keep their careers going well past 65 to, say, 70 or beyond.

If you're in this latter group, and if you're healthy enough to assume that you might be able to reach your goal of working longer, then this decision could make a big difference in how much risk you can keep taking with stocks into your 50s and 60s. Even a few more years of paid work will make a huge difference, not only on your ability to stay invested, but also on the long-run survival of your nest egg. How?

- For starters, working longer means you can *delay tapping your Social Security benefits,* and every year you delay that trigger increases the amount you can expect to receive from Uncle Sam every month once you do retire.

- It also means you *won't need to tap your retirement funds* to live on, since you're still collecting a paycheck. You'd be surprised at how letting your portfolio grow unfettered for five additional years can turn a questionable retirement into a comfortable one. For instance, assume that you have $700,000 amassed in your nest egg at age 62, and you plan on working until you're 67. If you don't need to withdraw money from your nest egg at 62 and can instead let it keep growing, in five years that sum will balloon to nearly $900,000 even if you were to assume a modest rate of return of 5 percent a year.

- Remember too that if you're still working, you will also be helping the cause by *continuing to put new savings into your retirement plan.* So instead of depleting your portfolio, you can add to it, potentially making up for any shortfalls you face. Assuming you and your spouse make, say, $100,000 annually, and you save 15 percent of your paychecks every year, even five more years of work can add $75,000 in actual savings, not counting investment returns.

- And finally, because workers can afford to take more risks than retirees, it will allow you to *keep more of your portfolio in equities,* which could theoretically grow the pot even faster.

Your actual retirement is only one consideration of time horizon. Another is the question of how long your retirement will actually be. Because a person who makes it to 65 years of age has a statistically good chance of surviving to 85, if not 90, you have to plan to keep growing your money well after you retire. While you may not want to keep the majority of your portfolio in equities after you quit working, the fact that you have to keep your money growing—and outpacing inflation—for a quarter century means that you must be willing to have a decent exposure to equities for a longer time than is commonly expected.

Your Risk Tolerance

Risk tolerance simply refers to your emotional capacity to handle volatility and risk. Ultimately, the right mix of stocks and bonds for you will depend not only on your time horizon, but also on your own sensibilities. Do you consider yourself a **conservative** investor, who's fearful of losing even 10 to 20 percent of your portfolio's value in any short stretch? Would suffering such a loss cause you to undo your long-term plans and sell? Or are you a more **moderate** risk taker, willing perhaps to lose as much as 20 to 30 percent in a bad market in exchange for capturing most of the potential gains of stocks? Or are you an **aggressive** investor, with the emotional fortitude to withstand a 30 or even 50 percent loss in any single bear market, since you have your eyes on the long-term prize?

Failing to gauge your own true appetite for risk can be dangerous. After all, accepting a strategy that's too risky for your taste not only can turn out to be counterproductive, but you could wind up in a worse situation than if you had played it a bit too conservative all along.

For instance, assume that you were advised to hold 80 percent in equities and 20 percent in fixed income, even though you'd be much more comfortable with a moderate 60 percent stock / 40 percent bond mix. Now, assume this is 2008, and the stock market has just plunged 37 percent (while bonds gained 5 percent). With an 80 percent stock / 20 percent bond mix, you'd be looking at losses of 29 percent, meaning that your original $100,000 portfolio would have shrunk to $71,000. Upset by how much you lost, you might sell out of equities and move entirely to bonds, missing out on the stock market recovery in 2009 that sent the S&P 500 index up 26.5 percent. The result: by the end of 2009, your original $100,000 would be at $75,600.

Now let's assume that you stayed true to yourself and played it safe, keeping 60 percent in stocks and 40 percent in fixed income. You still would have lost money in 2008, but your portfolio would have stayed above $80,000. If the more moderate loss was enough to keep you in equities in 2009, then your strategy would have paid off, as an original 60 percent stock / 40 percent bond mix would have returned your portfolio to $92,000 by the end of that year.

A good way to know if you're capable of handling a particular weighting in equities is to go back to 2008 as well as the crash of 2000–2002 to see if you were comfortable enough with your allocation to hang on. If you panicked and acted on that emotion, you have to reexamine whether your portfolio is right for you.

Investors who know exactly what type of risk tolerance they have—but who do not want to implement a strategy on their own—can turn to risk-based asset allocation funds that many mutual fund companies offer. For example, Vanguard LifeStrategy Growth is designed for aggressive investors and keeps about 80 percent of its assets in equities. Vanguard LifeStrategy Moderate, with around 60 percent exposure to equities, is for moderate investors. And Vanguard LifeStrategy Conservative, with only around 40 percent in stocks, is for the conservative set. Unlike target date retirement funds, though, these types of asset allocation funds maintain the same risk level over time. So as you get older and your sensibilities shift from aggressive to moderate to conservative, it's up to you to downshift into the more conservative options.

Your Savings and Wealth

The whole point of keeping a majority of your investments in stocks during your working years is to make sure your portfolio can outpace inflation. Equities help you do that because they grow so much faster than other asset classes. Investing in stocks, though, isn't the only route to ensuring that your nest egg will grow aggressively.

Saving is an even surer bet. To be sure, investing gains generated by equities are like "found money," and there's probably a sense of satisfaction that comes from knowing that your money is working for you. But there are times in the market when you can't count on stocks to do the heavy lifting, in which case you'll have to do that work for yourself (Figure 4-2).

FIGURE 4-2 Expected Annual Returns
Combinations of savings levels and portfolio returns that will get you to about $1 million in 25 years.

Annual Savings	Annual Returns	Balance in 25 years
$10,200	10%	$1,003,140
$11,900	9%	$1,007,940
$13,700	8%	$1,001,550
$15,900	7%	$1,005,660
$18,300	6%	$1,004,020
$21,000	5%	$1,002,270

For instance, say you're currently saving $10,000 a year into your retirement account, and you have a 25-year time horizon. Let's further assume that you've crunched the numbers and determined that to live a comfortable retirement, you'll need to amass $1 million in that time. To get there, you'd have to earn slightly more than 10 percent a year on your money, which means that if history is any guide, you'd have to be extremely aggressive—bordering on having to keep nearly 100 percent of your money in stocks.

Want to be able to dial down that equity exposure? Well, historically, a 70 percent stock / 30 percent bond allocation has delivered annual gains of around 9.3 percent a year since 1926. To still make it to $1 million in 25 years, you'd simply have to boost your annual savings to around $11,300.

Is that still too aggressive for your taste? Then if you can manage to set aside $12,000 a year—in other words, if you can boost your original savings amount by 20 percent—than you could dial back your allocation to a mere 50 percent stock and 50 percent bond weighting. Want to be even more conservative than that? Well, if you can increase your savings a tad more, to $13,000 a year, you could go to just 30 percent stocks and 70 percent fixed income and still be able to reach your goal of $1 million, based on the long-term historic performance of that mix (Figure 4-3).

Like savings, wealth is another component that must be factored into your planning. For instance, a middle-class saver who makes an average annual salary

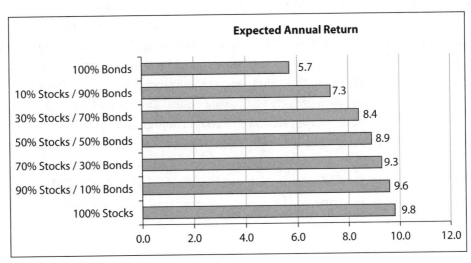

FIGURE 4–3 Expected Annual Returns
Expected annual returns based on various asset allocation strategies.

and has no pension to rely on nor a trust fund for support requires growth in his or her portfolio. That investor must make sure that the combination of savings and investment appreciation creates a retirement fund that's sufficient to pay for living expenses throughout a retirement that could potentially last 30 years or longer.

On the other hand, a wealthy investor may not require so much growth to make the numbers work. For instance, a person with, say, $5 million may not need to put that much in stocks if his or her goal is simply to fund a comfortable retirement. That's because even if that $5 million were mostly invested in bonds and some dividend-paying stocks that collectively yield 4 percent, that person would be able to generate $200,000 in income—without any capital appreciation—simply because of the original value of the account.

Of course, the vast majority of us have far less to work with, which means our portfolios need to do some of the heavy lifting for us.

Start Simple: Age-Based Rules

Two age-based rules can be used to calculate what your optimal asset allocation.

The 100-Minus Rule

Historically, the most common way investors determined what their basic asset allocation should be was by using their age as a proxy for how much they ought to hold in fixed income. The idea here is, if you're 20 years old, you ought to keep 20 percent of your money in bonds and the remaining 80 percent in equities. At 40, your allocation should shift to 60 percent stocks and 40 percent fixed income. Because of this basic math, this rule is sometimes referred to as the "100-minus" rule, since 100 minus your age gets you to your equity allocation (Table 4-1).

This back-of-the-envelope rule served a couple of important purposes. First, it helped investors understand that early in their investing careers, they needed to be far more aggressive with their portfolio than they planned to be toward the end of their working days. Moreover, it showed investors that their asset allocation policy needed to be dynamic. That is to say, over time your investing strategy needs to gradually change in nature. And in this case, change means to downshift.

Within the financial planning world, this downshifting effect is sometimes referred to as a **glide path**. That's because like a plane that starts off high in the sky and gradually descends toward a landing, you must dial down your equity exposure to reflect the change in your age, time horizon, and in many cases risk tolerance.

The trouble is, as Americans began to work longer and as they began to live longer into retirement, planners and asset managers began to question whether the 100-minus rule was too conservative. This isn't necessarily the case early on, when this rule calls for 20-somethings to have 80 percent of their money in stocks. But if you follow the rule to a T, at 50, you would keep only half your portfolio in equities. Yet from an actuarial perspective, 50-somethings need their money to last for potentially 40 more years.

TABLE 4–1 The 100-Minus Rule *The classic rule for allocation based on age*	
Age	**Allocation**
40	60% stocks / 40% bonds
45	55% stocks / 45% bonds
50	50% stocks / 50% bonds
55	45% stocks / 55% bonds
60	40% stocks / 60% bonds
65	35% stocks / 65% bonds
70	30% stocks / 70% bonds
75	25% stocks / 75% bonds
80	20% stocks / 80% bonds
85	15% stocks / 85% bonds
90	10% stocks / 90% bonds

The 110- and 120-Minus Rules

As a result, this rule of thumb has been slightly tweaked over the years. In the late 1990s, for example, when stock investing grew in popularity and aggressiveness was rewarded, some in the financial planning community created a variation to this rule called the 120-minus rule. This rule called on 20-somethings to keep 100 percent of their money in stocks. Meanwhile, 50-year-olds were routinely told that they should feel comfortable having as much as 70 percent of their holdings in equities.

To this day, several target date retirement funds, which allocate money for investors, maintain this level of aggressiveness for investors who are just 15 years from retiring. The T. Rowe Price Retirement 2030 fund, for instance, which is geared for such workers, keeps around 75 percent of its assets in equities (there will be more on target date funds later on).

In the aftermath of the financial crisis, though, conventional wisdom shifted once more. Many older workers in the Great Recession began to worry about their job and investment security. They grew hesitant to remain so aggressive, especially so close to retirement. As a result, the personal finance community adjusted this age-based rule once more, and now conventional wisdom recommends something called the 110-minus rule, which splits the difference (Table 4-2).

Using this calculation, 30-year-olds should keep 80 percent of their money in equities and 20 percent in bonds. Meanwhile, a 50-year-old would do best to maintain a 60 percent equity / 40 percent fixed income weighting.

TABLE 4–2 The 110-Minus Rule
A newer rule for allocation based on age

Age	Allocation
40	70% stocks / 30% bonds
45	65% stocks / 35% bonds
50	60% stocks / 40% bonds
55	55% stocks / 45% bonds
60	50% stocks / 50% bonds
65	45% stocks / 55% bonds
70	40% stocks / 60% bonds
75	35% stocks / 65% bonds
80	30% stocks / 70% bonds
85	25% stocks / 75% bonds
90	20% stocks / 80% bonds

Basic Allocation by Life Stage

The constant adjustments being made to the age-minus rules highlight something important: Basic thinking about allocation strategies changes from time to time, and there's just as much art to establishing an investing strategy as there is science. At the end of the day, there are two important takeaways from these rules: First, you need to establish a glide path (though not necessarily one that requires you to make basic changes every year of your life). And second, you need to appreciate the basic concept that the more time you have to invest, the more you ought to be invested in stocks.

Broad-Based Model Portfolios

Your 20s to Mid-30s

The recommendation during your 20s to mid-30s is to have 80 percent stocks / 20 percent bonds (Figure 4-4).

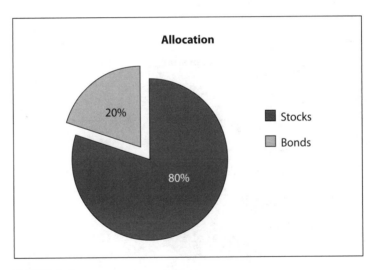

FIGURE 4–4 From Your 20s to Mid-30s

Characteristic: Aggressive growth, negligible income.

Return expectations: Compared with a 100 percent stock allocation, you give up only a slight amount of returns—around half a percentage point in annual returns, based on historic performance. Since 1926, a basic 80 percent portfolio delivered annualized gains of 9.4 percent, according to the Vanguard Group. And in the best year for this strategy, investors earned 45.4 percent in total returns.

Risk considerations: The 20 percent slug in bonds may not seem like much. But there are key benefits. First, it creates a portfolio that's slightly less volatile than a 100 percent allocation, based on standard deviation. Moreover, the single worst calendar-year loss for this allocation was a decline of 34.9 percent, which was around 8 percentage points less than the worst-year loss for a 100 percent stock portfolio.

Finally, the chances of losing money with this approach are slightly less than with a 100 percent stock approach. Over the past 87 years, for instance, a 100 percent stock allocation has lost investors money in 27 years. In other words, the odds of suffering a calendar-year loss with an all-stock strategy are about 29 percent. By comparison, an 80 percent stock / 20 percent bond mix lost money in two fewer years, meaning that the chances of losing money drop to around 26 percent.

Your Mid-30s to Mid-40s

The basic recommendation during your mid-30s to mid-40s is to have 70 percent stocks / 30 percent bonds (Figure 4-5).

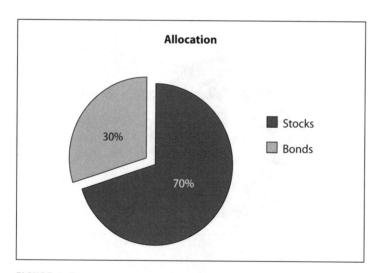

FIGURE 4-5 From Your Mid-30s to Mid-40s

Characteristic: Growth, modest income.

Return expectations: This strategy returned nearly as much as an 80/20 mix, posting annualized returns of 9.1 percent since 1926. And in its best calendar year, a 70 percent stock / 30 percent fixed income allocation delivered gains of 41.1 percent.

Risk considerations: In its best year, a 70 percent equity / 30 percent bond portfolio gained about 4 percentage points less than an 80/20 mix, and in its worst year, it lost roughly 4 points less—dropping as much as 30.7 percent. Moreover, this strategy lost investors money in one less year since 1926, bringing your chances of losing money with this strategy down in any single year to one in four, or 25 percent.

Once you start looking out over longer time frames, you start to see the real benefit of this more moderate approach. Over rolling five-year periods dating back to 1926—meaning that you would look at the performance from 1926 to 1930, then from 1927 to 1931, and 1928 to 1932, and so on—the absolute worst returns for a standard 70 percent stock / 30 percent bond mix was a loss of 6 percent. By comparison, an all-stock portfolio's worst 10-year run was a loss of nearly 13 percent. And the 70/30 strategy lost money in only 6 percent of the five-year stretches going back to 1926. Even better, a 70/30 portfolio has never lost money in any rolling 10-year stretch in history.

Not only are you likely to lose less money with a 70/30 mix than with more aggressive strategies, but you can expect to see a noticeable reduction in volatility. For example, a basic 70/30 mix exposes you to a portfolio, based on standard deviation, that's 29 percent less volatile than an all-equity strategy and 21 percent less risky than a 90 percent stock / 10 percent bond approach, according to Ibbotson.

Your Mid-40s to Mid-50s

The recommendation during your mid-40s to mid-50s is to have 60 percent stocks / 40 percent bonds (Figure 4-6).

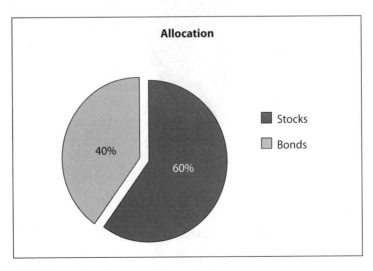

FIGURE 4–6 From Your Mid-40s to Mid-50s

Characteristic: Balanced risks, decent income.

Return expectations: Compared with a 100 percent stock strategy, this 60/40 mix may look somewhat tame, delivering annual returns of 8.7 percent since 1926. But compared with a 70 percent stock / 30 percent bond mix, this balanced strategy produces nearly as much in total returns. And its best calendar-year performance was nearly identical: around 37 percent gains versus about 41 percent for the 70/30 approach.

Risk considerations: With a 40 percent slug in bonds, the down years won't seem nearly as bad. In fact, the worst calendar-year performance for a 60 percent stock / 40 percent bond mix was a loss of around 26 percent, which is about half as bad as the more than 50 percent loss for an all-stock portfolio. Moreover, the odds of losing money in any single year for the first time drop below one in four, to 24 percent.

Your Mid-50s to Mid-60s

The recommendation during your mid-50s to mid-60s is to have 50 percent stocks / 50 percent bonds (Figure 4-7).

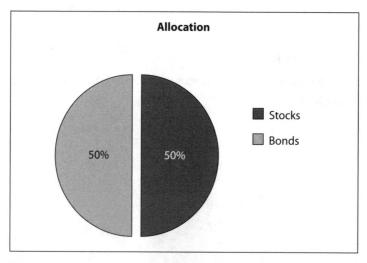

FIGURE 4-7   From Your Mid-50s to Mid-60s

Characteristic: Conservative growth, aggressive income.

Return expectations: The historic gain for a perfectly balanced portfolio, with half its assets in equities and half in bonds, is actually not that far from that of an 80/20 plan. This 50 percent stock / 50 percent fixed income allocation has delivered annualized gains of 8.3 percent over nearly a century, versus 9.1 percent for a 70/ 30 portfolio.

You have to look over longer time horizons to really appreciate how a 50 percent equity / 50 percent bond strategy can help you. Consider that over rolling 20-year periods since 1926, this strategy has returned around 15 percent annually during its best stretch, and 5 percent a year in its worst, averaging nearly 9 percent a year over two-decade time horizons.

Risk considerations: Once your bond weighting hits 50 percent, you really begin to see a reduction in risk in your investments. For starters, a 50/50 strategy has lost money in less than 20 percent of the calendar years since 1926. The worst 5-year stretch for such a strategy was a negligible loss of 2.8 percent, during the Great Depression years. And it has never posted a loss over a rolling 10-year stretch in history.

From a volatility standpoint, the average long-term standard deviation of a 50 percent equity / 50 percent fixed income portfolio stands at about 11, which means that this portfolio's ride is about half as bumpy on a day-to-day basis as is the performance of an all-equity strategy.

In Retirement

The recommendation in retirement is to have 30 percent stocks / 70 percent bonds (Figure 4-8).

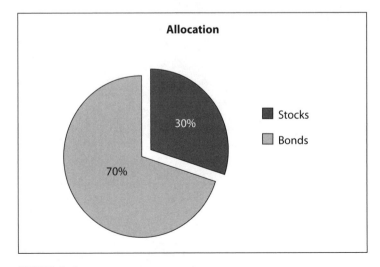

FIGURE 4–8 In Retirement

Characteristic: Safety and high income.

Return expectations: Well into your retirement, your goal isn't so much to grow your money, though you still need some capital appreciation. Instead, your major priority is to preserve your nest egg. A 30 percent stock / 70 percent bond portfolio has delivered average annual returns of 7.3 percent a year. That's nothing compared with the 10 percent you can get on stocks, but it's still 4 percent more per year than the historic rate of inflation. So you get some inflation protection.

   This strategy won't deliver blistering returns. In fact, the single best year for a 30/70 approach was a gain of 28 percent. Still, this 30/70 strategy has made investors money in every rolling 5-, 10-, and 20-year stretch in history.

Risk considerations: With 70 percent of your money in bonds, you get a portfolio that's only 45 percent as rocky as an all-stock strategy. Moreover, the worst single-year loss for this portfolio was a modest decline of 14 percent, during the Depression years.

   Held over longer periods of time, investors get even more portfolio protection. Consider that the worst-performance 10-year stretch for a 30 percent stock / 70 percent bond strategy was an annualized gain of 3.6 percent.

QUIZ

1. **The more time you have to invest, the less need there is to earn big returns.**
   A. True
   B. False

2. **Younger investors can afford to take risks with stocks because ...**
   A. They have less money to put at risk.
   B. They earn more money, so they can save more money.
   C. They have more time to correct market missteps.

3. **Because older investors tend to earn more money, they can afford to take more risks with their portfolio.**
   A. True
   B. False

4. **Though simplistic, the 100-minus rule is still useful because ...**
   A. It reinforces the notion that your portfolio needs to grow more conservative over time.
   B. It reinforces the notion that your portfolio needs to grow more aggressive over time.
   C. It instructs older investors to remain aggressive, which is needed given the long nature of retirement.

5. **An aggressive 80 percent stock / 20 percent bond portfolio has a ...**
   A. Greater than one in four chance of losing money.
   B. Worse than one in four chance of losing money.
   C. One in four chance of making money.

6. **The worst one-year loss for a 60 percent stock / 40 percent bond portfolio was ...**
   A. Twice as big as the losses for a 100 percent stock portfolio.
   B. Half as big as the losses for a 100 percent stock portfolio.
   C. The same as a 100 percent bond portfolio.

7. **A 50 percent stock / 50 percent bond portfolio is ...**
   A. Half as volatile as an all-equity strategy.
   B. A quarter as volatile as an all-equity strategy.
   C. Twice as volatile as an all-bond strategy.

8. **A 50 percent stock / 50 percent bond portfolio has never lost money over any five-year stretch in history.**
   A. True
   B. False

9. **A 30 percent stock / 70 percent bond portfolio has never lost money in any calendar year.**
   A. True
   B. False

10. **A 30 percent stock / 70 percent bond portfolio has never lost money in any five-year period in history.**
    A. True
    B. False

chapter 5

Subasset Allocation

Next, let's look at allocating within your asset classes.

Your Stocks

As was previously noted, the risks and returns you can expect from stocks will depend in part on what type of equities you're dealing with. The potential gains and losses, for instance, from owning shares of a fledgling company that has yet to turn a profit will likely differ from those holding the stock of a multinational giant that has turned a profit for the past 50 years. Similarly, owning shares of stocks in companies based in developing economies such as Indonesia or the Philippines will offer a different result, in many cases, from owning shares of domestic concerns.

What this means is that the types of stocks you use to implement your basic asset allocation plan can and will affect the risk and reward profile of your portfolio. This is a critical point because it means that you don't have to reduce or increase your overall exposure to equities to alter your portfolio's risk-adjusted returns. Instead, you can maintain your strategic split between stocks and bonds and just tweak the types of equities and fixed-income investments that you use to execute that plan.

When it comes to your equities, the trick is striking the right balance between your domestic large-cap and small-company stocks; between your American equities and your foreign holdings; and within your foreign stock portfolio between your mix of developed market stocks and emerging market shares.

Small Stocks Versus Large Stocks

The first major subasset decision to make is between shares of risky but potentially rewarding small-company stocks and stable but slower-growing large-cap shares. Over long stretches of time, small-company equities have been shown to slightly outperform blue chip shares. Blue chip stocks have posted annualized gains of 10 percent since 1926, versus nearly 12 percent for small-company shares.

But over any single calendar year or 5- or 10-year stretch, these two types of equities have taken turns outpacing each other. Indeed, large-cap stocks led the market in the 1950s, only to be overtaken by small-cap shares in the 1960s and 1970s. That was followed by an extended period of large-cap dominance in the 1980s and 1990s. Then since 2000, small-company shares have retaken the lead (Table 5-1).

The 1970s and 2000s offer a particularly vivid illustration of why it makes sense to diversify your equities among large and small stocks at all times. Both periods have generally been regarded as "lost decades" for U.S. stocks because the S&P 500 index lost value on a real, inflation-adjusted basis in both 10-year time periods. Still, it would be a mistake to say that investors did not make any money in equities during those tough years.

TABLE 5–1 Small Versus Large Stocks—Performance
Performance of small and large stocks by decade

	Small Stocks	Large Stocks
2000s	6.3%	–0.9%
1990s	15.1%	18.2%
1980s	15.8%	17.6%
1970s	11.5%	5.9%
1960s	15.5%	7.8%
1950s	16.9%	19.4%
1940s	20.7%	9.2%
1930s	1.4%	–0.1%
1920s	–4.5%	19.2%

Source: Ibbotson Associates

Small stocks, for instance, posted annualized gains of 11.5 percent throughout the 1970s, beating inflation by more than 4 percentage points a year. Similarly, from the end of 1999 to the end of 2009, large-company stocks went nowhere in nominal and inflation-adjusted terms. Yet throughout that stretch, small stocks returned a respectable 6.3 percent annually, again beating inflation by about four points annually.

While there are some general guidelines for guessing when small stocks are likely to shine and when large-cap stocks will outperform, it's difficult to predict with absolute certainty. As a result, investors are advised to maintain a permanent allocation to both.

But how much of your domestic stock portfolio belongs in each?

Target weighting in small stocks: 10 to 20 percent

Why? For starters, if you tally up the market value of all the publicly traded small companies in the United States as well as all the big ones, you'd find that small companies represent roughly 10 to 20 percent of the total value of the domestic equity market. So conventional wisdom says that's a good place to start. Why not add more, given the historic outperformance of small-cap shares? You could if you wanted to "tilt" your portfolio in a particular direction, and were willing to accept greater risk in your portfolio (which we will address in a later chapter).

But the fact is, balanced investors may not need more small stocks for diversification's sake, because large- and small-cap shares are generally well correlated with each other (Table 5-2). In other words, when one of them zigs, the other also zigs, though perhaps not to the same degree. That was certainly the case in the past several years. Both large- and small-cap stocks rose from 2003 to 2007 (in the bull market), but small did better than large. Then in the bear market of 2007 to 2009, both fell in lockstep—only large held up better than small. And since 2009, both have been rising in unison, though small is back to outperforming.

Also, there's a point at which adding more small-cap stocks to your domestic portfolio would noticeably increase your volatility. For example, a 90 percent large-cap / 10 percent small-cap domestic stock portfolio returned around 8.3 percent a year over the past 10 years, versus 7.4 percent for an all-large-cap stock strategy. Yet that 10 percent dose of small shares barely added any additional risk to the overall portfolio. Push that small-cap weighting to 40 percent of your U.S. shares, and volatility jumps by around 15 percent. Remember that your goal is to maximize your risk-adjusted returns, not just your absolute gains.

TABLE 5–2 Small Versus Large Stocks—Direction		
Small stocks and large caps often move in the same direction.		
	Large Stocks	**Small Stocks**
2007–2010	–0.3%	–0.5%
2003–2007	12.8%	17.3%
1995–1999	28.6%	18.5%
1988–1992	15.9%	13.6%
1980–1984	14.8%	21.6%
1970–1974	–2.4%	–11.1%
1960–1964	10.7%	11.4%

Source: Ibbotson Associates

Moreover, there are longer-term risks to consider. Over rolling five-year periods, the worst performance for small stocks was annual losses of 28 percent for five years. That's double the losses suffered by blue chip equities in their worst five-year stretch (Table 5-3).

TABLE 5–3 Small Versus Large Stocks—Lows		
Small stocks expose you to potentially lower lows.		
	Large Stocks	**Small Stocks**
Worst 1-year loss	–43.4%	–58.0%
Worst 5-year loss	–12.5%	–27.5%
Worst 10-year loss	–1.4%	–5.7%

Source: Ibbotson Associates

Domestic Stocks Versus Foreign Shares

Foreign stocks used to be considered exotic investments for U.S. shareholders. No longer. In this age of globalization, American investors have easy access to a global array of equities through mutual funds, exchange-traded funds, and even directly through their brokerage accounts.

Just as with small stocks, foreign shares and U.S. stocks are growing increasingly correlated, as global trade has erased some of the distinctions between the United States and other economies (Table 5-4). This means that when U.S. stocks fall, you can't necessarily count on foreign shares to move in the opposite direction. Defensive diversification, then, isn't really the goal. There are plenty of other reasons, though, to want to invest beyond American shores.

TABLE 5–4 Foreign Versus U.S. Stocks Returns *International equities often move in the same direction as U.S. stocks.*				
	U.S.	**Int'l**	**Asia**	**Europe**
2009	26.5%	32.5%	24.3%	36.8%
2008	−37.0%	−43.1%	−36.2%	−46.1%
2003	26.8%	39.2%	39.0%	39.1%
2002	−22.1%	−15.7%	−9.0%	−18.1%
2001	−11.9%	−21.2%	−25.2%	−19.6%
1999	21.0%	27.3%	58.0%	16.2%
1990	−3.1%	−23.2%	−34.3%	−3.4%

Source: Ibbotson Associates

For starters, the majority of global stocks—and global equity market capitalization—is found outside the United States these days (Figure 5-1). So by turning your back on international equities, you will be missing out on a majority of the world's companies and opportunities. Moreover, because foreign firms are based in economies that generate the vast majority of the world's gross domestic product, avoiding international investing altogether means that you will be underexposed to the economies that generate the lion's share of worldwide economic growth.

What's more, you will be underexposed to the faster-growing parts of the world, since the United States is a mature economy. Indeed, while U.S. GDP has been growing at an annual rate of 3 percent or less in recent years, worldwide GDP is growing at a much faster clip of more than 4 percent.

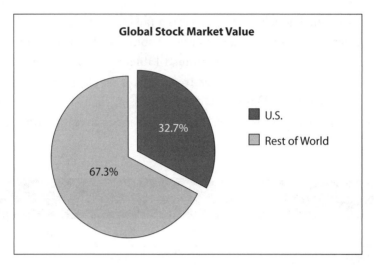

FIGURE 5–1 U.S. Versus the World
American equities account for a minority of the world's total stock market value.
Source: Bloomberg

Even if you don't get direct stock diversification by investing abroad, you do enjoy other forms of diversification through international equities. For instance, because foreign companies domiciled outside the United States transact the bulk of their business in euros, yen, and other currencies, you get currency diversification through international stocks.

And when it comes to currencies, the dollar does zig when other markers zag. In many cases, even if the U.S. and foreign stock markets move in lockstep, you can get wildly different results from your U.S. and foreign shares simply due to fluctuations in the underlying currencies of your equity exposure.

Target weighting: 30 to 40 percent of your equities

Why? If foreign stocks represent the majority of global market capitalization, why shouldn't they account for most of your equity exposure? Part of it has to do with the fact that as an American investor who will require U.S. dollars to fund your retirement costs, there are too many risks associated with exposing the bulk of your nest egg fund to foreign currency fluctuations. There's also the fact that gaining exposure to foreign stock funds is still relatively more expensive than investing in a U.S. fund.

Moreover, it boils down to volatility. While increasing exposure to foreign stocks ought to increase safety over time—because of stock and currency diversification benefits—there's actually a point of diminishing returns.

Researchers at Vanguard studied the utility of adding increasing amounts of foreign shares to a broad-based equity portfolio. Based on data since 1970, they found that as an investor's foreign weighting grows to 10 percent, then to 20 percent, and then to 30 percent, the overall volatility of that portfolio gradually declines. This happens whether you are adding foreign shares to a 100 percent stock portfolio, to an 80 percent stock / 20 percent bond portfolio, or to a 60 percent stock / 40 percent bond strategy. However, at around 40 percent of your overall equity exposure, foreign stocks actually begin to add incremental bumpiness to your portfolio's performance.

The study's author noted in the report that "the maximum historical diversification benefit would have been achieved by allocating approximately 40 percent of an equity portfolio to non-U.S. equities." What's more, Vanguard officials found that an investor can receive 99 percent of the maximum possible diversification benefit of foreign shares with an allocation capped at 30 percent international. Even a 20 percent weighting for foreign shares would deliver 84 percent of the potential diversification benefit.

Within Your Foreign Stock: Developed Markets Versus Emerging Markets

Emerging economies—led by dynamic economies in China, India, Russia, and Brazil—are among the fastest-growing markets throughout the world. In fact, China's economy has recently been expanding at four times the rate of the United States. What's more, emerging market stocks have delivered annualized gains of around 10 percent over the past 15 years, which is about two and a half times greater than the gains posted by companies based in Western Europe.

At the same time, foreign stocks in the developed world are heavily weighted toward Europe and Japan, whose economies were recently racked by debt and growing more slowly than the United States. Given this contrast, one would assume that conventional wisdom might call for allocating most of one's foreign exposure to the emerging world. But that's not the case.

Your target: 20 percent to 33 percent of your foreign equity holdings.

Why? For starters, while it's true that emerging market stocks have outperformed the developed world over the past 15 years, they haven't led the way in every calendar year during that stretch. In fact, in three of the past six years, the slower-growing developed world's stocks have beaten emerging market shares (Figure 5-2).

This dovetails with a lesser-known fact about investing: Stocks in faster-growing economies don't always deliver better results. Indeed, recent research by a team at the London Business School found that there is little or no link between the speed with which an economy grows and how well shares of companies based in that market perform. For instance, they looked at the behavior of Chinese equities over a much longer time period. Since 1985, China's economy grew two-thirds faster than the United States. Yet their research showed that since that time, American equities delivered around twice the returns of Chinese shares.

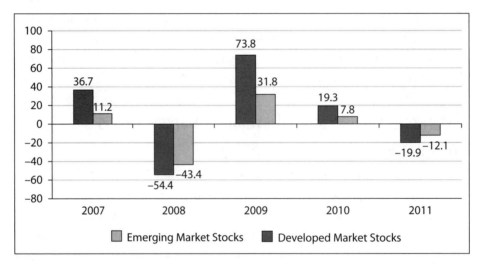

FIGURE 5–2: Emerging Versus Developed
Emerging markets either dramatically outperformed or underperformed the developed markets throughout the financial crisis.

Source: Morningstar

Another reason why investors must limit their emerging markets exposure is that these regions account for only about 20 percent of global market capitalization, while the economies in which these companies are based generate only about a third of all global economic output. Allocating a bigger share to emerging market stocks than their fundamental footprint would dictate is therefore hard to justify, especially given the added volatility they bring to a portfolio.

Emerging market stock funds, for example, sport a standard deviation of greater than 24. That's even riskier than U.S. small-cap stocks and is more than a third more volatile, based on standard deviation, than developed market shares. Indeed, in 2008, when the S&P 500 index of U.S. large caps fell 37 percent, and when the MSCI EAFE index of foreign developed market stocks sank 43 percent, emerging market equities lost more than 52 percent of their value.

Your Bonds

U.S. Government Versus Corporate Debt

There is a great debate today about how much of your U.S. bond portfolio ought to be in government debt and how much should be held in corporate securities. Based on the total amount of debt outstanding in the U.S. market, Treasury bonds and other government-related securities account for roughly 70 percent of the fixed-income universe, with corporates making up the other 30 percent. In fact, if you own a so-called total bond market fund, which offers you instant exposure to the broad domestic fixed-income market, that's about how the domestic portion of your bond portfolio would be allocated.

But some observers say this is wrong. With stocks, it makes sense to weight your portfolio based on aggregate market values because market cap rewards success in equities. For instance, the bigger a company gets based on the value that investors ascribe to it, the greater its sway on the movement of the stock market. So by holding stocks in proportion to market value, you tilt your portfolio to shares of the most successful businesses. In essence, you're riding winners.

With bonds, however, it's sort of the opposite. Fixed-income markets are weighted by debt, not market capitalization. Therefore, the more a government or corporation borrows, the more bonds it has on the open market, and the more likely it is that those securities will dominate investors' portfolios. Many critics argue that to weight your portfolio based on aggregate borrowing is to reward the losers, not the winners.

That's why these investors object to keeping 70 percent of U.S. bonds in government debt, since this is simply rewarding Uncle Sam for fiscal irresponsibility. They also object to underweighting corporate bond issuers who have worked hard to reduce their debt loads and have improved their balance sheets in recent years.

These contrarians argue that bond investors ought to make some adjustments. They say that you should disregard the value of all U.S. Treasury and government debt held by policy-making organizations around the world, ranging from the

Federal Reserve to the Bank of China. Why? They argue that those organizations are not buying up Treasuries based on investing motives. Rather, foreign governments and central banks purchase Treasuries and hold them for political purposes, and that should not affect how true investors allocate their fixed income.

If you strip away all U.S. government debt held by central banks, governments, and other political organizations, you're left with closer to a third in government debt and two-thirds in corporates.

The compromise: Most individual investors get their U.S. bond exposure through a diversified fund, such as a total bond market fund or an actively managed bond fund that holds several types of debt. These funds tend to keep anywhere from 50 to 70 percent of their assets in government debt, with the remainder going to corporates. By splitting your U.S. bond allocation and using half your money to buy a corporate bond fund and the other half to buy a total bond market fund, you'd be left with anywhere from half to two-thirds of your overall U.S fixed-income exposure in corporate debt. Having a balance makes sense, as interest rate risks are probably on the rise after a 30-year decline in market yields.

Domestic Versus Foreign

Another decision you'll have to make is how much of your fixed-income exposure ought to be held overseas. On paper, there are plenty of reasons to put a hefty dose of your fixed-income portfolio into non-U.S. debt.

For starters, not only do foreign bonds make up a majority of the total global debt market, but they are the single biggest asset class in the world financial markets. In dollar terms, they represent 37 percent of all investable assets, meaning that international bonds are collectively worth more than U.S. stocks, U.S. bonds, and foreign equities. Moreover, thanks to mutual funds and exchange-traded funds that are widely available to retail investors, foreign bonds are now easier to access—and cheaper to buy and sell—than at any time in history. As the Vanguard Group noted in a recent report, "Investors can now view global bonds as an accessible and viable asset class with the potential to reduce portfolio return volatility in a manner similar to the diversification benefit expected from international equities."

But there is a limit to the good that foreign bonds can bring to a portfolio. That's because international debt securities trade in non-U.S. currencies. And the added volatility that those currencies *contribute* to your portfolio begins to detract from the diversification benefit that international bonds can offer (Figure 5-3).

But aren't foreign stocks also susceptible to currency risk? Yes, but stocks are by nature bumpy to begin with. As a result, the incremental risk that foreign currencies add to international equities turns out to be quite small on a relative basis compared with the inherent volatility of stocks.

Vanguard recently studied the role that currencies play in international assets. Researchers there found that fluctuations in exchange rates account for only about 10 percent of the volatility of foreign stocks. However, when it comes to bonds, those currency moves have historically accounted for more than 60 percent of the volatility of foreign fixed income.

That might be acceptable to you if currency fluctuations also accounted for the lion's share of foreign bond returns. Unfortunately, they don't. Since 1985, Vanguard found, currency movements accounted for only a fraction of the returns generated by international bonds.

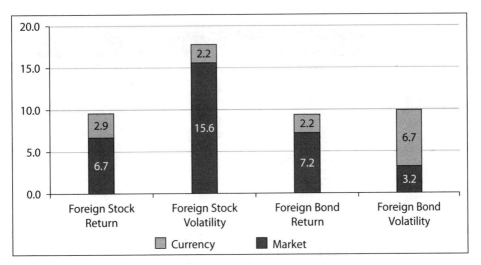

FIGURE 5–3 Market Versus Currency Risk
When it comes to bonds, international diversification adds more risk than returns.
Source: Ibbotson Associates

Target allocation to foreign bonds: 20 percent

Why? Vanguard studied a myriad of variations of globally diversified funds. In particular, researchers at the mutual fund company examined the risks and rewards of adding various levels of exposure to international bonds. This was based on a diversified portfolio consisting of 60 percent stocks (specifically, 42 percent in U.S. equities and 18 percent in foreign shares) and 40 percent in

U.S. bonds. In almost every case, adding even the slightest exposure to unhedged international bonds increased the overall volatility of this portfolio. However, assuming that around a third of your stock exposure is abroad as well, then limiting your foreign bond exposure to 20 percent seems to add the least amount of risk.

Your Strategic Plan

With these assumptions, let's revisit the strategic asset allocation strategies laid out in the prior chapter. In each case, the basic weightings between stocks and bonds are exactly the same, but the equity and fixed-income weightings have been subdivided further, reflecting the risks and rewards that core subasset classes offer (Tables 5-5 through 5-9).

TABLE 5–5 Mid-20s to Mid-30s: 80% Stocks / 20% Bonds

Overall 80% Stock

45% U.S. large-cap stocks

10% U.S. small-cap stock

15% foreign developed market stock

10% foreign emerging market stock

Overall 20% Bonds

15% U.S. total bond market

5% foreign bonds

Returns on 80/20 Mix

	80/20 Portfolio	100% Stocks
5-Yr. Annual Return	5.4%	9.1%
10-Yr. Annual Return	8.3%	7.5%
20-Yr. Annual Return	8.1%	8.2%

Risks on 80/20 Mix

	80/20 Portfolio	100% Stocks
Standard Deviation	13.6	16.2

TABLE 5–6 Mid-30s to Mid-40s: 70% Stocks / 30% Bonds

Overall 70% Stock

40% U.S. large-cap stock

10% U.S. small-cap stock

15% foreign developed market stock

5% foreign merging market stock

Overall 30% Bonds

25% U.S. total bond market

5% foreign bonds

Returns on 70/30 Mix

	70/30 Portfolio	100% Stocks
5-Yr. Annual Return	5.7%	9.1%
10-Yr. Annual Return	7.7%	7.5%
20-Yr. Annual Return	7.9%	8.2%

Risks on 70/30 Mix

	70/30 Portfolio	100% Stocks
Standard Deviation	11.6	16.2
Sharpe Ratio	0.22	0.19

TABLE 5–7 Mid-40s to Mid-50s: 60% Stocks / 40% Bonds

Overall 60% Stock

35% U.S. large-cap stock

5% U.S. small-cap stock

15% foreign developed market stock

5% foreign emerging markets stock

Overall 40% Bonds

30% U.S. total bond market

10% foreign bonds

(Continued)

TABLE 5–7 Mid-40s to Mid-50s: 60% Stocks / 40% Bonds   *(Continued)*

Returns on 60/40 Mix

	60/40 Portfolio	100% Stocks
5-Yr. Annual Return	5.3%	9.1%
10-Yr. Annual Return	7.4%	7.5%
20-Yr. Annual Return:	7.6%	8.2%

Risks on 60/40 Mix

	60/40 Portfolio	100% Stocks
Standard Deviation	10.0	16.2
Sharpe Ratio	0.24	0.19

TABLE 5–8 Mid-50s to Mid-60s: 50% Stocks / 50% Bonds

Overall 50% Stock

30% U.S. large-cap stock

5% U.S. small cap-stock

12.5% foreign developed market stock

2.5% foreign emerging market stock

Overall 50% Bonds

40% U.S. total bond market

10% foreign bonds

Returns on 50/50 Mix

	50/50 Portfolio	100% Stocks
5-Yr. Annual Return	5.5%	9.1%
10-Yr. Annual Return	6.9%	7.5%
20-Yr. Annual Return	7.4%	8.2%

Risks of 50/50 Mix

	50/50 Portfolio	100% Stocks
Standard Deviation	8.4	16.2
Sharpe Ratio	0.27	0.19

TABLE 5–9 In Retirement: 30% Stocks / 70% Bonds

Overall 30% Stock

17.5% U.S. large-cap stock

2.5% U.S. small-cap stock

7.5% foreign developed market stock

2.5% foreign emerging markets stock

Overall 70% Bonds

60% U.S. total bond market

10% foreign bonds

Returns on 30/70 Mix

	30/70 Portfolio	100% Stocks
5-Yr. Annual Return	5.4%	9.1%
10-Yr. Annual Return	6.1%	7.5%
20-Yr. Annual Return	6.9%	8.2%

Risks on 30/70 Mix

	30/70 Portfolio	100% Stocks
Standard Deviation	5.7	16.2
Sharpe Ratio	0.37	0.19

QUIZ

1. **Small stocks should be considered a core holding.**
    A. True
    B. False

2. **Small stocks represent 10 to 20 percent of total U.S. stock market value. Investors ought to keep ...**
    A. 10 to 20 percent.
    B. More than 20 percent.
    C. Less than 20 percent.

3. **Foreign stocks represent more than 50 percent of total global stock market value. Investors ought to keep this amount in international equities:**
    A. More than 50 percent
    B. 50 percent
    C. 40 percent
    D. 25 percent

4. **At what allocation do foreign stocks cease adding diversification?**
    A. 20 percent
    B. 30 percent
    C. 40 percent
    D. Never

5. **What is the reason for placing a cap on total foreign equity allocation?**
    A. To reduce volatility
    B. To reduce potential gains
    C. To reduce the potential for losses

6. **Compared with government bonds and high-quality corporate debt, high-yielding bonds are ...**
    A. Safer because they pay out more.
    B. Riskier because they have to offer high yields.
    C. Higher-returning investments than other corporate bonds.

7. **What amount of foreign bonds is ideal in your portfolio?**
    A. 20 percent
    B. 30 percent
    C. 50 percent

8. **International debt adds what to your portfolio?**
   A. Greater currency risk
   B. Greater portfolio volatility
   C. The chance for greater returns
   D. All of the above
   E. None of the above

9. **Which asset class represents the greatest share of total financial market value?**
   A. Foreign stocks
   B. U.S. stocks
   C. Foreign bonds
   D. U.S. bonds

10. **What is the biggest concern when it comes to investing in foreign bonds?**
    A. Political risk
    B. Interest-rate risk
    C. Credit risk
    D. Currency risk

chapter 6

Making Tactical Adjustments and Tilts

Broadly speaking, there are two schools of thought when it comes to asset allocation. On the one hand, there are those buy-and-hold investors who believe that it is too difficult to try to anticipate changes and trends that are taking place in the market. Therefore, why even try? These investors believe that the most important decision that you ought to make is establishing your long-term **strategic asset allocation plan**—in other words, setting a mix of stocks, bonds, and other assets that's appropriate for you given where you are in your life cycle. Then, come back to tweak that basic blueprint only when there are sufficient changes in your age, time horizon, risk tolerance, or overall level of savings and wealth to justify making an adjustment to your plan.

Since a strategic investment strategy is by definition long term in nature, short-term fluctuations in market conditions or changes in economic trends ought not to matter, this school of thought argues. Market conditions should not influence you to stray from your plan. Moreover, even if you believe that there are immediate opportunities to be had or risks to be avoided in the market—say you think that green energy stocks are about to take off, or you think that because of new laws and policies, certain healthcare stocks are bound to rebound, or you think that that stocks are getting way too expensive and want to reduce your exposure—you should remain disciplined and hold off from upsetting your long-term plan. After all, whether certain segments of the market are about to suffer or thrive does not change your basic risk profile. If you're 60 years old and only 5 years off from retirement, you have certain capital appreciation and preservation needs that are immutable.

On the other hand, there are asset allocators who believe just as strongly in the importance of establishing a long-term strategic plan, but these investors think that there are certain additional needs that investors might want to satisfy. Moreover, there are certain opportunities that the market may be presenting that can be incorporated into an asset allocation plan by making a few targeted adjustments. These types of tweaks are referred to as **tactical shifts**.

A classic example of a tactical asset allocation strategy would be one that reflects a market-timing decision that an investor seizes upon. For example, in early 2009, the stock market's average price/earnings ratio—based on a specific calculation of earnings (popularized by Yale economist Robert Shiller) that averages out corporate profits over a 10-year period—had fallen to its lowest level in more than two decades. Historically, when stocks trade at below-average price/earnings ratios, they tend to perform better than their historic average over the subsequent 10 years (and conversely, when they trade at above-average P/E ratios, they tend to perform worse than their long-term average in the coming decade). This goes back to the notion of assets reverting to their historic mean. Sure enough, from March 2009 to March 2013, stocks went on a bull run that more than doubled the value of domestic equities.

Obviously, making tactical adjustments to your asset allocation plan requires more work on your part. For starters, if you are making an adjustment based on a market call, you are responsible for doing the due diligence on the research. You are responsible for paying attention to the trend long enough to know when that opportunity has come and gone. And you are responsible for adjusting your asset allocation plan back to its original mix once you believe that the circumstances that called for the tactical adjustment are no longer present.

How to Make Tactical Shifts

In general, there are three basic procedures for making a tactical shift in your plan.

Option 1: Change Your Broad Weightings

Obviously, the easiest thing you can do is to alter your basic mix between core stocks and bonds.

For example, history shows that there are basic back-of-the-envelope ways to gauge the long-term future performance of stocks and bonds. When it comes to Treasury bonds, the technique is absurdly simple. Just take the current yield on a 10-year Treasury. Whatever that figure is—in 2013, 10-year Treasuries were paying investors about 2.5 percent in interest—that is what your average annual return for Treasuries is likely to be for the next decade (Figure 6-1). In other words, even though long-term Treasuries have historically delivered total returns (income plus capital appreciation) of 5.7 percent a year since 1926, this current yield indicator is forecasting that your Treasury securities are likely to deliver less than half of that over the next 10 years.

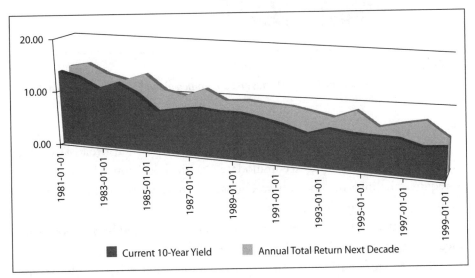

FIGURE 6–1 Forecasting Treasuries
The current yields on 10-year Treasuries forecast total returns for the next 10 years.
Data is for January 1 of each year. *Source:* Ibbotson Associates

So assume that you want to make a tactical shift within your bonds holdings because you believe them to be overpriced. Let's go back to that 60 percent stock / 40 percent bond portfolio we referred to in the previous chapter. Using broad-based weightings, you can simply choose to dial down your exposure to government bonds given the circumstances. Here, you might trim your weighting in government bonds by a small amount—say, 5 or 10 percentage points—and redeploy those funds into an asset class that you believe to be relatively cheaper than Treasury debt. In this case, that might warrant converting that 60 percent stock / 40 percent bond mix into a 65 percent equity / 35 percent fixed income portfolio or a 70 percent stock / 30 percent bond mix (Figure 6-2).

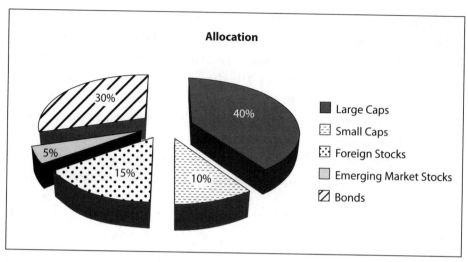

FIGURE 6–2 Option 1

If you're 60% stocks / 40% bonds and are worried about Treasuries, you could shift more to stocks.

Of course, not all investors are comfortable using such broad strokes to adjust their strategic plan to accommodate a tactical decision. Moreover, doing so requires the investor not only to choose when to apply the tactical adjustment, but also to pay close enough attention to determine when that tweak is no longer warranted because market conditions have shifted once more. Often, once you make the initial decision to tactically tweak your allocations, deciding when to shift back to a more neutral stance that relies solely on your strategic decision making can be even harder than the original call. In that case, there are other ways to go about implementing your tactical allocation moves.

Option 2: Change Your Suballocations

Rather than upset your overall mix of stocks and bonds, a more targeted approach would be to use your subasset weightings to make your adjustments. In other words, maintain your overall mix between stocks and bonds, but within the equity portion of your portfolio, tweak your exposure to large, small, foreign, and emerging market shares. And within your fixed-income portfolio, tweak your blend among government, corporate, and foreign securities. While this will have a slight impact on your overall risk-reward profile—since any additional returns you are seeking in almost every circumstance have to be paid for by adding some additional risk—it will represent far less of an adjustment than using your broad asset classes to make these shifts.

How would this work? Let's go back to that 60 percent stock / 40 percent bond example from the prior chapter. As you'll recall, in that moderate mix, your stocks are really divided in a couple of ways. You have 40 percent of your equities in domestic shares and 20 percent in foreign. Then within your domestic stock portfolio, 35 percent goes to large caps and 5 percent goes to small caps. And within your international equity holdings, 20 percent is held in developed market shares and 5 percent is in emerging markets. Your fixed income is similarly divided. Within your 40 percent bond weighting, 30 percent is held in a mix of U.S. government and corporates, and 10 percent goes to international fixed income.

Now, let's assume that, for a variety of reasons, you want to reduce your exposure to Treasuries because you think they are overpriced. But you want to do so without undoing your larger mix of stocks versus bonds. In that case, you might choose to reduce your 30 percent weighting in U.S. bonds. But instead of shifting that money to stocks, you would simply redistribute it to other areas of fixed income—in this case to your foreign fixed-income holdings. The result would still be an overall 60 percent stock / 40 percent bond weighting. But within your fixed income stake, your mix would now be 25 percent U.S. government and corporate debt, with 15 percent in foreign bonds (Figure 6-3).

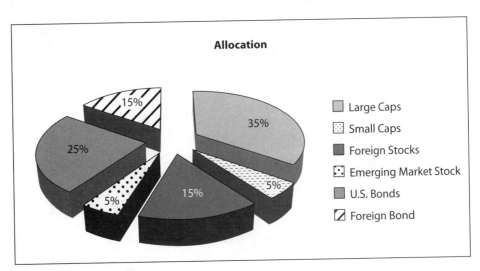

FIGURE 6–3 Option 2
You could maintain your 60% stocks / 40% bonds strategy and just tweak your mix of bonds.

Option 3: Think Core and Explore

Popularized by the brokerage firm Charles Schwab, the phrase "core and explore" refers to dividing your portfolio into two separate buckets that work in a hub and spoke fashion. The first—and most important—part of your strategy would be your "core" holdings. This bucket would hold the vast majority of your assets, in many cases around 90 percent. And you would use your long-term strategic asset allocation plan to implement this part of your strategy. So there's not a lot of tweaking you should be doing in that part of your portfolio.

Say you're a moderate-risk investor. You might choose to keep 60 percent of this bucket in stocks and 40 percent in bonds. You would then maintain this strategy for this bucket no matter what changes take place in market conditions. The only thing that should get you to change the mix of stocks and bonds here is if your own circumstances change—for instance, if you get older, your risk tolerance changes, or your savings rate changes.

Then you would turn to the "explore" part of your portfolio. This part, which would hold around 10 percent of your money, is the bucket that you would use to implement any tactical change or basic market tilt that you want to entertain (Figure 6-4). Let's go back to our example. Assume again that your goal is to reduce your stake in government bonds for the next several years—fearing that these investments are overpriced and are expected to deliver below-average returns going forward. While maintaining your overall 60 percent stock / 40 percent bond

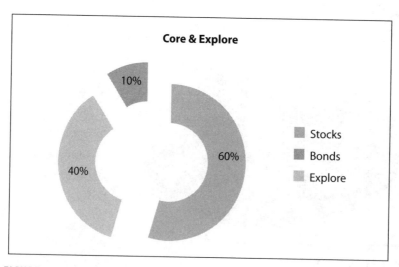

FIGURE 6-4 Option 3
You could also view your portfolio as two separate entities.

mix in your core bucket, the explore part of your portfolios would be used to invest in other forms of cheaper income. In that case, you might take half the explore bucket and use it to invest in foreign bonds and corporate bonds. And you could take the other half to invest in dividend-paying stocks.

Common Tactical Moves

There are two kinds of tactical moves that you can apply within your asset allocation strategy. Style tilts seek to take advantage of inefficiencies that may exist in the market. Other adjustments can be used to respond to market trends or to meet a specific financial need.

Style Tilts

There's a certain irony when it comes to investing. Asset allocation is considered vital because the markets are generally thought to be efficient, meaning that it's difficult for superior research or stock selection skills to bring about greater risk-adjusted rewards. However, history has shown there to be a few areas in the market where inefficiencies do exist. In those cases, investors can earn a premium by tilting their asset allocation strategies to take advantage of those anomalies. In other words, strategic asset allocation works because the markets are efficient. But where there are inefficiencies, there are tactical asset allocation strategies that you can employ to take advantage of them.

The Value Tilt

The first area of opportunity is within the realm of so-called value stocks. These are shares of overlooked or underappreciated companies that are being punished by investors with a low price/earnings multiple or other valuation gauge. In some cases, value stocks might be underpriced because of missteps that management made. In others, it may be that investors are simply paying more attention to flashier, faster-growing companies that are stealing the market's attention.

In either event, history has shown there to be a premium that investors can earn over very long periods of time by focusing on these unloved stocks. As Benjamin Graham, considered the father of value investing, noted in *The Intelligent Investor*, "If we assume that it is the habit of the market to overvalue common stocks which have been showing excellent growth or are glamorous for some other reason, it is logical to expect that it will undervalue—relatively, at least—companies that are out of favor because of unsatisfactory developments of a temporary nature. This may be set down as a fundamental law of the stock market, and it suggests an investment approach that should prove both conservative and promising."

History has borne this out. Since 1928, the average large value stock has produced annual gains of 10.8 percent a year, which is nearly a percentage point greater annually than the broad market and more than two percentage points better than high-priced growth stocks. Among small-company shares, this value advantage is even more pronounced (Figure 6-5).

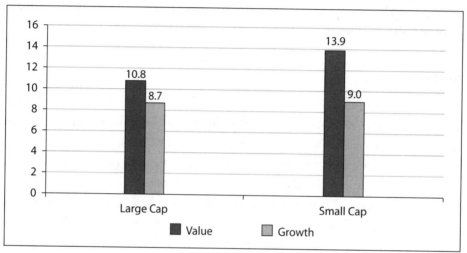

FIGURE 6–5 The Value Advantage
Value-oriented shares of all sizes have outpaced growth since 1928.
Source: Ibbotson Associates

Now, there will be times when value investing falls out of favor, as was the case from around 1994 to 1999, when high-priced but fast-growing growth stocks beat value for five straight years. So you wouldn't want to tilt your portfolio so much toward value that you would totally miss out on those momentary periods of growth outperformance. But because the price you pay for your investments ultimately influences your future performance, lower-cost value stocks should have a long-term advantage.

Implementation: If you're using your subasset allocation, creating a value tilt can be as simple as you make it. In our 60/40 model portfolio, you'll recall that 40 percentage points of that 60 percent stock weighting are held in domestic stocks.

And value represents half of the broad large- and small-cap markets. If you wanted to increase that, you could take half your domestic allocation and put it into **value-oriented stock funds**—such as the iShares Russell 3000 Value ETF, which encompasses value stocks in both the large- and small-cap markets. The resulting mix between your broad-based domestic funds and your value-oriented funds would give you an aggregate 75 percent weighting in value and 25 percent in growth.

You can also use the core and explore method to accomplish the same thing. In that case, you could simply have a standing 10 percent position in your "explore" bucket in a value-stock fund like the Russell 3000 Value ETF. Or you could split between funds that specialize separately in **large-cap value** (like the Vanguard Value fund) and **small-cap value** (such as the Fidelity Small-Cap Value fund) (Figure 6-6).

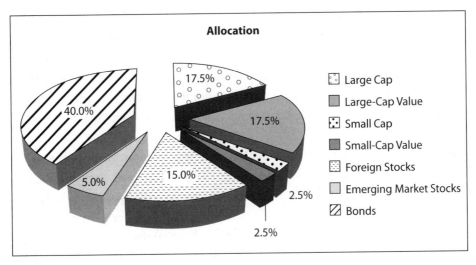

FIGURE 6–6 Value Tilt
You can use your suballocations to boost your exposure to value stocks.

Small-Stock Tilt

It's a well-known fact: the smaller the market capitalization of a stock, the better its chances of delivering better-than-average long-term gains. Part of this has to do with scale: small stocks can grow their earnings a lot faster than large, established businesses can. Moreover, smaller companies are still followed by fewer analysts than are large blue chip shares. So they any market inefficiencies exist that allow stock pickers to gain an advantage, they would most likely be found within the small-company realm.

TABLE 6–1 Advantage of Being Small *Small stocks have consistently beaten large caps over 20-year rolling periods.*		
	Large Caps	**Small Caps**
1991–2010	9.1%	13.5%
1972–1991	11.9%	14.6%
1953–1972	11.7%	13.8%
1934–1953	10.7%	14.6%

Source: Ibbotson Associates

Finally, it boils down to the historic relationship between risk and reward. Small stocks expose investors to greater risks in a number of ways. For starters, the odds are greater that small companies will fail and go out of business compared with larger, more established blue chip firms. Moreover, small companies are much more volatile than large companies. Indeed, the average standard deviation for a small stock is nearly 32, versus 20 for a large-cap company. That means that smaller companies are more than 50 percent more volatile than large-company shares.

Implementation: Using your subasset classes, you can simply increase your exposure to small-company stocks while maintaining your overall equity allocation. For instance, in typical 60/40 portfolio where 40 percent of your stocks are held domestically, the strategic plan calls for dividing that between 35 percent large and 5 percent small. You could simply peel off about 10 percent from your large-cap exposure, creating a domestic portfolio that's about 25 percent in blue chip shares and 15 percent in small (Figure 6-7). Within a core and explore model, you could simply take that additional 10 percent tactical bucket and use it to invest in additional small-cap stocks or funds, such as the Vanguard Small-Cap Index fund.

Low-Volatility Tilt

As small stocks show, the relationship between higher-risk assets and the potential for higher reward can be strong. However, there are exceptions to every rule, and there's one big one when it comes to stocks.

Shares of companies exhibiting below-average volatility have historically outperformed high-volatility stocks. In this case, the specific type of volatility

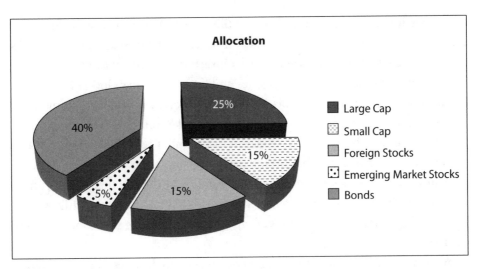

FIGURE 6-7 Small Tilt
You can use your suballocations to boost your exposure to value stocks.

we're talking about is beta, which measures how investments move in correlation with the broad market. Low-volatility stocks often have a beta of 0.70 or lower, meaning that if the broad market were to fall 1 percent, these stocks are likely to drop around a third less in value. Conversely, if the market were to rise by 1 percent, low-volatility stocks would be likely to gain around a third less than the market as a whole. Yet over the past 1, 5, 10, 15, and 20 years, low-volatility stocks have managed to outperform the S&P 500 index. In fact, over the long run, low-volatility shares—despite the fact that they gain less in up markets—have beaten the S&P 500 by a little less than 2 percentage points annually (Table 6-2).

TABLE 6–2 Low Volatility, High Returns *Stocks with low beta have beaten the broad market consistently over time.*		
	Low-Volatility Stocks	**S&P 500**
5-Yr. Annual Return	4.7%	2.0%
10-Yr. Annual Return	7.0%	4.1%
15-Yr. Annual Return	8.8%	6.1%
20-Yr. Annual Return	10.4%	8.6%

Source: S&P

How is it possible, then, that low-volatility stocks perform so well? Part of it has to do with the value premium. Academic research shows that high-beta stocks have a tendency to be overpriced because investors incorrectly assume that high volatility will automatically deliver better and faster gains than low volatility will. Meanwhile, the fact that low-volatility shares are often overlooked by momentum-driven investors who are looking to turn a quick profit means that these types of equities tend to be neglected, which in turn implies that they are likely to be undervalued by investors. This means that low-beta stocks win in part because they are cheap. And their advantage is compounded by the fact that investors have a tendency (incorrect though it may be) to overpay for highly volatile shares, believing (again incorrectly) that there's an advantage to doing so. So low-volatility equities win in both cases.

Also, because low-volatility stocks tend to actually lose less value in market downturns as well as plain-vanilla down months for stocks, they don't have to make as much in good times to stay ahead of high-beta stocks. Regardless of the reason, low-volatility shares are among the best stocks when it comes to risk-adjusted returns.

A popular way to measure that is to use something called the Sharpe ratio. Created by Nobel laureate William Sharpe, a finance professor at Stanford, this tool gauges how much return an investment delivers per unit of risk. In other words, this measure tells you how much you're being paid to take risk. The higher the Sharpe ratio, the better an investment is regarded in risk-adjusted terms. And over the past 20 years, the Sharpe ratio for low-volatility stocks is around twice as high as that of the S&P 500 index (Table 6-3).

TABLE 6–3 The Low-Volatility Advantage
Low-volatility stocks strike a good balance between risk and reward.

Sharpe Ratio	Low-Volatility Stocks	S&P 500
3-Year	2.3	1.4
5-Year	0.3	0.1
10-Year	0.5	0.1
15-Year	0.5	0.2
20-Year	0.6	0.4

Source: S&P

Implementation: Using your subasset classes, you can take half your current domestic allocation and use it to invest in low-volatility stocks or stock funds. For instance, in that 60/40 model portfolio, 40 percent is in broad-based domestic stocks (split with 35 percent in large and 5 percent in small). Now, divide that weighting down the middle, leaving half where it is, and use the other half to invest in a large-cap low-volatility fund such as PowerShares S&P 500 Low Volatility ETF (17.5 percent) and SPDR Russell 2000 Low Volatility ETF (2.5 percent) (Figure 6-8). If you're using your explore portfolio, you can use it all to invest in low-beta stocks. But here too, you can split that between large- and small-cap low-volatility strategies, with around 8 percentage points of that core portfolio going to blue chip low-beta stocks and the remaining 2 percentage points going to a small-cap version of this strategy.

Market and Economic Developments

Tactical adjustments aren't limited to hidden premiums found in the market. Sometimes an investor seeks to make a tactical shift in his or her portfolio to satisfy a specific financial need. Other times, it's to take advantage of an emerging market trend that is currently transpiring. Or perhaps you feel the need to guard against a certain development that's taking place now in the general economy or financial markets. Or sometimes, you just feel the need—based on other

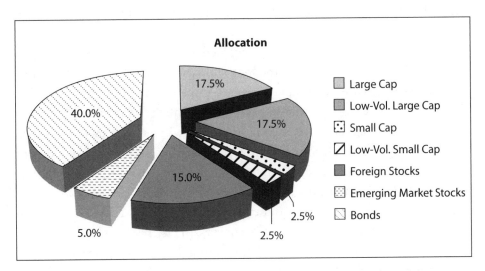

FIGURE 6–8 Low-Volatility Tilt
You can use your suballocations to boost your exposure to value stocks.

uncertainties that are taking place in your life—to play some defense when it comes to your portfolio.

Under any of these circumstances, investors can make small tactical adjustments without upsetting the balance of their strategic plans. In some cases, it simply means making a minor adjustment to your overall mix of stocks and bonds. In other cases, it means relying on some subassets while forgoing others to fit the circumstances. In still other cases, it may require adding a small weighting—perhaps 5 or 10 percent of your total strategy, perhaps in the form of your "explore" portfolio—to strike a slightly different balance that's better suited for your particular needs.

Among the most common tactical shifts are the following.

To Fight Inflation

For investors, maintaining the purchasing power of their portfolio is a constant goal. So inflation is the long-term enemy for investors. Yet there are periods in the economy when inflation doesn't simply threaten investors over the long run, it really begins to attack their portfolios in the here and now.

The long-run average rate of growth for inflation is around 3 percent, but in several periods in history, the consumer price index rose at well above double that rate—and in some cases even routinely grew by double-digit rates over several years. Most recently, this took place in the "stagflation" years between 1974 and 1982. But inflation also flared up as the economy expanded in the late 1960s, in the post–World War II boom of the mid- to late 1940s, and in the five-year stretch that ran just before the Great Depression, from 1917 to 1920.

Now, equities have generally been regarded as the one major asset that can hedge inflationary pressures over the long run, since, historically, equity returns have outpaced inflation by a rate of around three to one. And that's true. Yet many investors question whether stocks are sufficiently good at guarding against inflation in the short run. Case in point: in the high-inflation years of the 1970s, equities averaged 5.9 percent annually. On paper, that may seem like a decent gain, but it actually turned out to be a worse return than risk-free cash delivered. Worse still, inflation was growing at an annual rate of 7.4 percent throughout that decade, so that means that you ended up *losing* about 1.5 percent, in real inflation-adjusted terms, by investing in equities. In fact, research has shown that in short-term periods of severe inflation throughout history, stocks around the world have tended to lose value, in real inflation-adjusted terms, at about a 12 percent annual rate.

Yet there are other **alternative assets** that you can add to your explore portfolio to help mitigate the effects of inflation.

Commodities

What are commodities? These are raw materials that can be traded in bulk. Industrial commodities include "hard" items like steel, copper, nickel, and other unfinished or unprocessed goods that manufacturers require for factory production. They also include oil, natural gas, and other energy supplies that are used in the manufacturing process.

Commodities aren't just limited to hard goods. Agricultural or "soft" commodities include items such as wheat, corn, soybeans, and cotton that are used in the manufacturing process and traded on exchanges.

Hard and soft commodities can be purchased indirectly through shares of companies involved in the mining, harvesting, or processing of commodities. Or the actual commodities themselves can be held directly, though that can be more complicated and costly (as you would be responsible for storing and insuring tons of raw materials). The most convenient way of having direct ownership of commodities is through an exchange-traded fund that in turn owns and stores the actual materials for you. There are also funds that give you exposure to commodities through futures contracts that give you the right to buy or sell certain commodities at an agreed-upon later date at agreed-upon prices.

Historically, commodities have performed better than other assets during short-term inflationary spikes. Indeed, as Table 6-4 shows, commodities proved to be a great hedge against inflation in the years when the rate of inflation

TABLE 6–4 Commodities *How commodities performed in years with the biggest change in inflation*			
Year	**Large-Cap Stocks**	**Long-Term Gov't Bonds**	**Commodities**
2009	26.5%	−14.9%	18.3%
1987	5.2%	−2.7%	22.1%
2011	2.1%	28.2%	−5.3%
2004	10.9%	8.5%	17.6%
1999	21.0%	−9.0%	31.1%

Source: Ibbotson Associates

accelerated the most (though not necessarily when the rate itself was at the highest actual peak).

Why? Well, for starters, inflation is a phenomenon of rising prices. And when prices throughout the economy are climbing—perhaps because demand for goods and services is improving, or because the money supply in the economy is shrinking—that tends to boost the cost and value of raw materials that go into the industrial process. Moreover, you have to remember that a bet on commodities is generally a bet on the economy, since demand for many basic raw goods goes up when the economy improves, consumers buy more things, and factories must produce more things.

If commodities are such a good bet on the economy, why not own a small portion of them in your strategic plan? Well, for starters, you already do have some direct and indirect exposure to commodity producers when you buy stocks. For example, the biggest company based on market value in the S&P 500 index is ExxonMobil, whose biggest products are oil, gas, and natural gas, which are commodities. In fact, about 5 percent of the index itself is in basic materials stocks or in shares of companies that mine, smelt, or refine commodities. Of course, there is a slight difference in the nature of the stock of a commodity-producing company (whose value can rise or fall based on strategic decisions made by management in addition to the ups and downs of the underlying commodity prices).

Another reason to limit your exposure to commodities is that unlike other basic assets—like stocks and bonds—there's only one way to make money through this asset class. The price of the commodity has to rise. While stocks and bonds offer the possibility of income and capital appreciation, commodities limit your gains just to prices. So if you go through an extended time when the commodities you hold go nowhere in price, you won't make anything on your investment.

Older investors who frequently worry about an eventual short-term spike in inflation—and who often have other sources of income in their portfolio—can put roughly 5 to 10 percent of their portfolio (for instance, using your explore portfolio) in commodities. A modest weighting like that can actually reduce some of the volatility in your overall portfolio. That's because commodities have historically been only modestly correlated with stocks and bonds.

Gold

Gold is a very specific type of commodity. While there are some industrial applications for gold, this precious metal is more often used for consumer purposes as well as an inflation hedge for portfolios should the value of the dollar weaken. The reason is that investors look to the most recent period of sustained double-digit inflation—in the 1970s, when gold shined.

From 1975 to 1980, for instance, gold gained about 40 percent in value a year on average at a time when stocks delivered less than 10 percent. So gold can be an effective asset during short-term bouts of extreme inflation. Many investors do, in fact, put a small slug of the precious metal into their tactical portfolios whenever there are any signs of inflationary pressures forming in the economy.

The longer-term story is a bit muddier. While gold bugs love to talk up how well gold thrived in the face of 1970s-style hyperinflation—which is true—the fact remains that the metal's long-term record of outpacing inflation is very questionable. For starters, since 1975, gold prices have gained only about 2 percent a year, compared to the nearly 11 percent annual returns posted by large-cap stocks.

Moreover, over the really long term—since 1900—gold has managed to eke out real inflation-adjusted gains of only 1 percent annually. This means that not only is gold a poor way to stay ahead of long-term price spikes, but it's actually worse in long-term inflation-adjusted gains than even bonds, which have beaten inflation by 1.7 percentage points annually throughout history. In fact, gold has done about as good a job at beating inflation over extremely long stretches of time as has cash, according to research by London Business School professors Elroy Dimson, Mike Staunton, and Paul Marsh. In other words, it has not done that good a job at all.

TIPS

Historically, investors turned to commodities and stocks to try to outpace inflation because those were the best tools available to do so. In more recent years, the government has created a new device you can use to combat inflation using your fixed-income portfolio. Treasury Inflation Protected Securities, or TIPS, are a type of Treasury bond whose value cannot be ravaged by inflation. Like a normal Treasury bond, TIPS come with a fixed interest rate. But TIPS come with a built-in inflation kicker. With a regular Treasury bond, investors at maturity get the value of the original note back in full. With TIPS, though, the principal value of the note is regularly adjusted to reflect inflation as measured by the consumer price index. In other words, if inflation were to rise 3 percent, the underlying value of your TIPS bond would be increased by 3 percent.

The income you can expect, then, will also get a slight adjustment, though indirectly. While the original coupon rate is fixed, the amount of actual income you get is calculated by multiplying that rate by the underlying value of the bond.

Here, as the principal rises, your income goes up even though the coupon is fixed. Individual TIPS bonds can be purchased directly from the Treasury through its website Treasurydirect.gov. Or these bonds can be purchased through a bond fund that specializes in these inflation-adjusted securities.

Like other Treasuries, these bonds are not risk free. True, they are free of credit risk, since they too are backed by the full faith and credit of Uncle Sam. However, like an ordinary Treasury bond, TIPS can lose value if market interest rates rise, and the price that investors are willing to pay for older TIPS on the secondary market can fall. Investors can avoid that risk by buying individual TIPS and holding them to maturity.

If you're looking to brace your portfolio for an oncoming spike in prices, then TIPS can be used to replace a portion of your regular Treasuries and/or the other high-quality bonds in your portfolio.

To Seek More Income

Seeking to boost the level of income you generate from your balanced portfolio? Since 1926, dividend income has been responsible for more than 40 percent of investors' overall total returns. In more recent years, though, the contribution of dividends has fluctuated considerably. In the 1990s, for example, the vast majority of an investor's total gains came from capital appreciation. In the lost decade of 2000–2009, however, the only gains that investors saw came from the income that stocks threw off.

While the contributions of income to total returns tends to ebb and flow, for older investors who require income to fund their retirement expenses, income is a constant need. In recent years, income has been hard to come by, because market interest rates have fallen to near-record lows. Still, even in low-rate environments, there are tactical steps you can take by adding a small allocation to certain assets.

Real Estate Investment Trusts

Real estate investment trusts (REITs) are companies that own and manage investment properties. There are a variety of types of REITs whose shares are publicly traded with other stocks. Some specialize in office buildings, others in shopping malls, apartment buildings, industrial warehouses, or healthcare facilities. Regardless, the structure is virtually the same. For tax reasons, REITs must pass along to their shareholders at least 90 percent of the income they generate in the form of rents.

As a result, the yield you earn on a REIT or REIT fund is often higher than the dividends that stocks pay and is competitive with bond yields. In recent years, in fact, REIT income has actually exceeded bond income because of the low rate of bond yields. In the summer of 2013, for example, the average REIT was yielding around 3.5 percent. By comparison, 10-year bonds were paying out only around 2.5 percent, while the dividend yield on the S&P 500 was around 2 percent.

Not only that, but REITs have returned around 11.9 percent annually since 1972, which is around 2 percentage points better than stocks (Figure 6-9). So not only have they recently been yielding more than bonds, but they have produced better recent capital gains than equities. Plus REITs have a low correlation with the movements of stocks and are actually negatively correlated with bonds, which means that when one zigs, the other is apt to zag. Thereby, decreasing the volatility of your overall portfolio.

So why not invest more of your money in REITs? For starters, you already do invest in REITs if you own exposure to a broad-based S&P 500 fund. Of the 500 companies in the S&P, 17 are real estate investment trusts. So you already own REITs. Plus, if you own a home or other real estate outside your portfolio, you also have exposure to real estate in that form. The idea of using your explore portfolio—rather than your core—to introduce a small exposure to this alternative

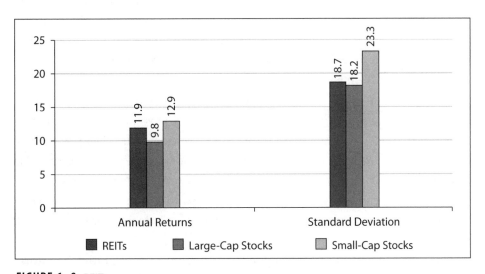

FIGURE 6–9 REITs
The risk and rewards of real estate investment trusts since 1972
Source: Ibbotson Associates

asset is to give you a slight boost in income and diversification without being overly weighted toward a single sector of the market (in this case real estate) that generates less than 10 percent of the total output of the U.S. economy.

Dividend-paying stocks

The vast majority of large-cap stocks routinely pay dividends, but dividend seekers tend to gravitate to a couple of special kinds of income-producing equities.

First, there are the high-dividend payers, those shares that throw off income of around 4 percent or more, roughly double the current dividend yield on the overall S&P 500. The allure of high-dividend payers is clear—they simply pay more right now than other stocks do. And that higher income offers a form of insurance for stock investors who aren't confident whether equities can deliver the type of capital appreciation that they have historically. Traditionally, high-income stocks have been found in certain areas of the market. Among them are the utility sector, consumer staples, healthcare, and financials.

High-dividend payers, though, come with a specific risk. A stock's yield is a function of two factors: the share price and the dividend payments per share that the underlying company makes. That means that while some stocks have a high yield because the company simply pays out higher-than-average dividends per share, other high payers sport bigger-than-average yields because their share prices have taken a beating lately, which artificially boosts the yield. That means investors must be particularly mindful of risks when investing in high yielders. After all, a plummeting share price is a sign that investors are worried about the financial strength of a particular company, and the risk is that a financially strapped business may not be able to sustain its current level of dividend payments—or dividends at all—in perpetuity.

The other type of dividend stocks that income investors seek out is those that yield only a modest amount today, but whose payouts have consistently grown over time. These dividend growers are considered less risky bets than high yielders. That's because their yields are modest now, which points to a relative degree of price stability for that company. Moreover, businesses that have proven to be able to grow their dividends year in and year out over decades are typically big, successful industry leaders with a long track record of financial health.

This makes dividend growers a good target of more conservative investors. While the trade-off for lower risk is lower current yield, historically those dividends rise quickly as payments grow consistently over time. Companies in the Standard & Poor's Dividend Aristocrats Index, for instance, have consistently boosted their payouts every year for at least 25 years. Moreover, dividend-growing stocks have actually outperformed others on a total return basis. Since 1981, stocks that have consistently raised their payouts have returned 10.3 percent annually, versus 7.6 percent for companies that pay dividends but don't routinely raise them and 1.6 percent for shares that pay no dividends at all

Cash

Like bonds, cash accounts offer investors a decent source of yields. But unlike bonds, which also offer the possibility of capital appreciation, cash accounts don't change in principal value. That's the good news. Over the past 82 years, cash accounts have posted a positive return in every year. The bad news is that you can really make money in cash in only one way, which explains why this asset has historically paid less than bonds. Indeed, since 1926, Treasury bills (a proxy for cash) have returned 3.6 percent annually, compared with nearly 6 percent for bonds. Worse still, on an inflation-adjusted basis, cash has returned only 0.6 percent annually in real terms.

Yet cash can still play an important role in creating income. For starters, because cash protects your principal to an even greater degree than do bonds, older investors who are nearing their time horizon can shift a small percentage of their money out of bonds and into cash for added capital preservation. Cash serves other purposes too. It happens to be a convenient parking place for investors to move money into, on a temporary basis, if and when they can't find good opportunities to buy other assets. This allows investors to protect capital while researching other options. Cash can also serve as a funding source for new ideas. Many investors will keep a small portion of their portfolio, say 5 percent, in cash so that they can immediately put money to work in new ideas that crop up, without having to sell out of their existing investments.

1. **Tactical asset allocation requires investors to ...**
   A. Undo their strategic allocations.
   B. Go against their strategic allocations.
   C. Neither.

2. **Tactical allocation decisions are by definition short term in nature.**
   A. True
   B. False

3. **By using subassets to make your tactical bets, you do not change the risk-reward profile of your portfolio.**
   A. True
   B. False

4. **You can make tactical adjustments to your portfolio through your ...**
   A. Asset classes.
   B. Subasset classes.
   C. None of the above.
   D. All of the above.

5. **Value stocks outperform because they are ...**
   A. Popular among investors.
   B. Higher priced by nature.
   C. Overlooked.

6. **Small-cap stocks expose you to greater risk. Therefore they ought to deliver ...**
   A. Higher returns than large stocks.
   B. Lower returns than large stocks.
   C. The same returns as large stocks.

7. **Low-volatility stocks are lower risk and they deliver ...**
   A. Lower returns than the broad market.
   B. The same returns as the broad market.
   C. Higher returns than the broad market.

8. **In years that witnessed the biggest increases in inflation, which asset class performed the best?**
   A. Commodities
   B. Stocks
   C. Bonds

9. **Because they are income-producing investments, REITs are more correlated with …**
   A. Bonds.
   B. Stocks.
   C. Commodities.

10. **If you're seeking to boost income, a natural place to turn is:**
    A. Commodities
    B. REITs
    C. Small-cap stocks

chapter 7

Alternative Approaches and Assets

Conventional asset allocation theory holds that since you age gradually over time, and since your time horizon and risk tolerance are apt to lessen gradually as well, your asset allocation decisions should follow a gentle downward trajectory—a "glide path," if you will—as if it were an airplane that begins its journey above the clouds at the 30,000-foot level and then gradually descends toward an eventual landing well into retirement. In fact, target date life-cycle funds, which help investors automate their asset allocation planning (and which will be discussed in Chapter 9), have literally turned to describing their changing asset allocation patterns as a gentle glide path that begins from one's youth and slowly descends into retirement and well past it.

For years, this has been an accepted rule when it comes to asset allocation. And for the most part, it still is. Yet increasingly, alternative theories have been cropping up—posed by financial planning experts and academics—that claim to reset the basic assumptions of retirement investing. On the face of it, some of these ideas seem quite logical, while others may appear quite risky at first. While there's not been enough time or research—and industrywide acceptance—to feel confident that these theories can stand the test of time, they are good to be aware of, especially if you want to incorporate some of the underlying ideas beneath them.

Leverage and Life-Cycle Investing

Of all the alternative theories of investment planning, this one appears the most provocative, because it introduces the notion that individual investors of all income levels should try to use leverage to boost their financial portfolios.

Origins

Leverage refers to the investing of borrowed funds to increase the impact of potential gains earned in the market.

It sure sounds risky, since if you lose on investments with borrowed funds, you must repay the debt—and cover the losses. But the underlying ideas behind the theory, put forward by two professors at the Yale School of Management, Ian Ayres and Barry Nalebuff, are actually quite intriguing because, at the very least, they highlight a flaw with conventional investing patterns.

The Basics

Ayers and Nalebuff have pointed out a big problem with the pattern in which we invest. Yes it's good that workers tend to invest in small increments over time—for instance, with every paycheck contribution to a 401(k) or IRA. And yes, that incremental investment pattern adds to diversification, since you are not only diversifying over different asset classes but diversifying the time periods in which you are making your investments as well. And that adds to safety.

But the fact remains that in your 20s and early 30s, when you are most likely to be able to tolerate risk in your portfolio—and therefore can take your chances with growth through stocks—you're likely to have the least money in absolute dollar terms to invest in such a risky way.

Think about it. When you are in your 20s and 30s, you're likely to have little savings already built up. And you're probably just starting out in your career. That means you're likely to make a modest annual salary. Even if you were an aggressive saver and socked away 10 percent of your pay every year, at a modest salary of, say, $40,000 a year, you'd be able to sock away only around $4,000 a year toward your portfolio. In other words, even if you were aggressively positioned for equities and invested 90 percent of your savings in the stock market, 90 percent of $4,000 would still come out to just $3,600 in actual investments.

Now fast-forward to when you're 60. By that time, you may be earning a much heftier salary of, say, $100,000 a year. And by that stage of your life, you may have socked away considerable amounts, possibly $750,000 or so, for retirement. Yet even if you were a conservative investor at this stage, socked away 10 percent of your salary each year toward your portfolio, and invested only half that money in stocks, that would mean that $5,000 of your new investments annually would be going into equities. That's more in dollar terms than the $3,600 you were investing in equities as an aggressive youth, even though your allocation is a much more conservative 50 percent stocks and 50 percent bonds. Moreover, half of your $750,000 in accumulated savings, or $375,000, would also be in stocks.

The bottom line: In dollar terms, you have the least amount of money going into equities in your youth even though your allocation, on a percentage basis, is most heavily weighted toward stocks.

Their solution: To even out the amount of money that you invest over the course of your life, young investors ought to leverage their portfolios—sometimes by a factor of as much as two to one—to boost their equity exposure early on. In other words, if you're planning to invest your annual savings of $4,000 a year, not only should all $4,000 go into stocks, but you should use leverage to gain as much as $8,000 exposure to equities.

You can gain that leverage in many ways. For instance, you can borrow money through a margin loan at your broker to buy the additional equity exposure. Or you can use LEAPS—which are options contracts that give you the right to buy exposure to broad indexes such as the Standard & Poor's 500 index at a later date at a certain price—to simulate the impact of a leveraged position. Or these days you can also use a levered fund that gives you exposure to various stock market indexes such as the S&P 500, but will deliver twice the gains (and, of course, potentially twice the losses) of the market depending on which direction stocks are headed in.

The Risk

Obviously, this is a risky strategy, since if you borrow on margin to invest in stocks and make a losing bet—for instance betting on equities on January 1, 2008, just before equities were about to lose nearly 60 percent of their value—you'll be out the value of your holdings, and you'll owe money on the margin loan. Even if you aren't using margin debt, the misfortune of bad timing early in your investing career can set you back considerably. For example, in a normal correction in which stocks lose around a third of their value, you could be looking at losses of 66 percent or more if your equity stake is levered two to one.

Still, Ayres and Nalebuff counter that they've analyzed actual market data going back to 1871. What they discovered was that their leveraged approach consistently outperformed other basic asset allocation strategies. For example, they compared this leveraged approach against the so-called 110-minus rule, the common asset allocation strategy that calls for you to subtract your age from 110 and put the resulting figure in equities. As a reminder, the 110-minus rule starts investors off reasonably aggressive (at 20, you'd have 90 percent in stocks, while at 30, that exposure would drop to 80 percent) and by the end becomes relatively conservative (at 65, you'd have 45 percent in stocks).

But the professors note that their method, as risky as it sounds, resulted in account balances that ended up 14 percent larger, on average, than the traditional 110-minus rule. And they argue that even in the worst-case scenario since 1871, their approach led to account balances that were about 3 percent larger than the 110-minus rule.

Moreover, the professors told *Money* magazine that the higher risk that's called for is precisely the type of risk that really young investors can take. After all, if a 20-something were to invest $5,000 a year in equities and lose the bulk of that in a bear market, he or she would still have 40 years and the ability to earn hundreds of thousands of dollars in lifetime salary to recover from a few thousand dollar loss up front. Moreover, they argue, investors need to keep in mind that taking more leverage in their really early years of investing will allow them to grow their money sufficiently to take less risk with equities when they are older and have real money to invest. For instance, they pointed out in *Money* magazine that "an investor starting at 200 percent stocks at 23 and tapering down to 32 percent at 67 can expect the same average return as a conservative investor who held 50 percent in stocks the whole way. Yet the range of lifetime outcomes is narrower in the leveraged portfolio—the highs aren't as high, but, crucially, the lows aren't as low."

In their book, *Life Cycle Investing: A New, Safe, and Audacious Way to Improve the Performance of Your Retirement Portfolio*, Ayres and Nalebuff explicitly state,

> *Our point is not to encourage risk taking—quite the contrary. Buying stock on margin when you're young reduces long-term risk because it allows you to do a better job evening out your otherwise lopsided exposure to the market. If you have $4,000 of market exposure when you're twenty-five and $200,000*

when you're sixty-five, it would be better to bring the initial exposure up to $8,000 and reduce the final exposure to $196,000.

They went on to note,

Proposing leverage often sets off red flags. Recent events highlight the issue. Young investors who followed our advice would have lost 64 percent of their savings in 2008. What does that say about our strategy? While losing 64 percent of your investments is never fun, it is much better to do so when you're twenty-five than when you're sixty-five. This is true for two reasons: First, you have a lot more time to adjust in response. Over the next forty years, you can work harder, save more, or consume less. Second, even following our advice, you'll have a lot less money in the market when you are twenty-five compared to when you are sixty-five.

Human Capital and Asset Allocation

Another alternative asset to consider is human capital.

Origins

Behavioral finance and personal finance expert Moshe Milevsky recently popularized a simple notion when it comes to assessing one's portfolio of assets. He noted in his recent book, *Are You a Stock or a Bond? Create Your Own Pension Plan for a Secure Financial Future*, that in addition to the stocks, bonds, and hard assets you own (such as real estate), there is one major asset class that is all too often overlooked: your ability over time to earn an income.

And that ability to earn income—along with the potential amount of that income, the expected volatility of that income, and the uncertainty of that income— must all be factored in when assessing your overall asset allocation plan.

The Basics

Milevsky argued in his book that "the single most precious asset on your personal financial balance sheet is not your savings account, your investment portfolio, your jewelry, or even your house. Rather it is the discounted value of all the salary, wages and income you will earn over the course of your working life."

He went on note that "this asset is called human capital, and though its precise numerical value might be hard to obtain and difficult to calculate, the fact remains that it's the best asset you have until well into your middle ages."

He's right. Think about when you were in your 20s. At that stage of life, chances are you didn't own a home yet. You may have started a 401(k) retirement plan, but your account balance was probably in the thousands, not the tens of thousands let alone hundreds of thousands. You probably didn't have any expectation of getting access to a defined benefit guaranteed pension. You may not have had life insurance. In fact, you may have had more money in your car than in your stock portfolio. In that phase of life, your human capital—that is to say, your ability to earn an ever-rising amount of income over the course of the next forty or fifty years—was the biggest thing going for you.

Even in your 40s, there's a strong likelihood that your future stream of income will still account for the vast majority of your personal finance balance sheet, as you could be looking at a quarter century of additional work earning you potentially $100,000 a year, or $2.5 million in pay. Yet in your mid-40s, you're probably not sitting on a portfolio worth more than $2.5 million. Only when you reach your mid-50s and 60s does your human capital start to be balanced out by your investable assets. And of course, by your mid-60s and 70s, human capital starts to dissipate as you get ready to retire.

The idea of human capital—and the underlying importance of investing in one's education and other credentials to ensure higher income later in life—has been around for years. But Milevsky and other behavioral economists have taken this idea and connected it to asset allocation planning.

How does it connect? For starters, just as you weigh the risk of any assets you hold—stocks, bonds, and real estate, for instance—you have to factor in the volatility of your potential income stream.

Here's a classic example: Say you're an academic who has tenure at a well-funded university with a large endowment, and through your employment, your retirement income is covered through a guaranteed pension. In this situation, you have a lot of certainty regarding your finances. First, you know you have job security through tenure. So no matter how bad the economy is, your immediate income is safe. You're probably also assured of obtaining routine cost-of-living adjustments over time because the university's finances are in good health. Your pension offers you a modicum of security because your basic retirement income needs will be met by your employer.

Well, what does that certainty provide you with? At the very least, it grants you the financial security that allows you to take more chances with the smaller portion of your personal finance balance sheet: your portfolio.

For example, because you have access to a secure pension, you can feel more comfortable investing in equities. After all, a pension is very much like a bond in that it promises you a set amount of interest income over time, through a vehicle in which your employer (not you) assumes the investment risk. Knowing that you have a bondlike asset on your balance sheet—and knowing that your employer has the financial strength of a high-quality bond issuer—should give you comfort to take on risk by investing the bulk of your own portfolio in equities.

There's another reason why, in this scenario, you'd have greater comfort investing in equities. Let's assume the stock market enters into a bear market. You know that in a bear market, you could easily lose a quarter of the value of your portfolio. If you have such a high degree of job security, though, you know that you could suffer occasional setbacks like this from time to time with relative ease. Why? Because you know that if push came to shove, you could always take advantage of the one asset that wasn't affected by the downturn—your income—and boost your savings rate for the next few years to make up that lost ground.

Plus, a steady paycheck would also let you keep your portfolio intact—in other words, there would be no need to sell to cover your day-to-day financial needs. That in turn would allow you to remain invested in stocks in hopes of enjoying the fruits of any subsequent recovery.

Now, let's change this scenario a bit. Let's assume that this is 2007, on the eve of the global financial crisis. Let's assume that you earn the same income as in our prior example, but in this case, you're not a university professor. Instead, you're a mortgage broker whose job is threatened by the housing meltdown. What's more, your exact pay is not known at the start of each year because your compensation is largely based on commissions. So depending on the economy and the season you're in, you could see wild fluctuations in the amount of your take-home pay.

Knowing what you know now, there's no way you'd feel comfortable being 100 percent exposed to equities as a mortgage broker in 2007, right? After all, stocks in 2008 sank nearly 40 percent. If you were certain that you'd lose your job in the same economic downturn that sent stock prices crashing, you probably would not expose your portfolio to such steep potential losses. After all, if you did get laid off, you'd have to sell some of your holdings to pay your bills, further depleting a portfolio that had already fallen by 40 percent.

What does that tell you? You could have two similarly aged professionals earning the same amount in salary with the same sized portfolios who each—based on the volatility of their human capital—may choose drastically different approaches to their asset allocation plans. In the case of the professor, he or she may choose to be 100 percent in stocks even at 40 or 50 simply because of the "bondlike" certainty of his or her income and the clarity of the risk. On the other hand, the mortgage broker may be uncomfortable investing more than half of his or her money in equities given that his or her income stream is much more "stocklike"—that is to say, it's high risk and highly unpredictable.

The Risk

All of this would seem to make sense—on paper. The trouble is, factoring human capital into your asset allocation decision making is much harder than it sounds. In fact, it is much more of an art than a science.

Sure, at the extremes, it would be easy to know that a person with 100 percent job security and retirement security could take 100 percent risks with equities. But in the real world, few of us have jobs that grant us that certainty of risk and that clarity of income. Many of us go through life with a perceived notion of how secure our jobs are. For some of us, those perceptions prove to be true. For others, however, they do not. So when a bad economy, a downturn within an industry, or risks that are specific to just your employer manifest themselves, your assumptions of job security can be tossed out the window.

That said, there is information you can work with. For instance, ask yourself if you work in an economically sensitive sector. Those would include sectors such as industrials, technology, financials, and energy. Jobs in these parts of the economy are more susceptible to riding high when the economy is good and falling when the economy is bad. In other words, these would be more stocklike. Then, ask yourself how healthy your own employer is. This is something you can easily tell based on general trends in hiring and layoffs. Also—and this is something that is probably the easiest to ascertain—assess how volatile your pay truly is. Does your annual income fluctuate more than 25 percent a year in either direction, due to new business or the lack thereof? Or is your income more bondlike, in that the amount of pay is highly predictable and certain?

Once you arrive at a general sense of whether your income tilts more toward equities or fixed income in characteristic, then you can use that information to tilt your own asset allocation strategy based on your circumstances.

A Rising Glide Path

Another way to look at asset allocation is to use the concept of a rising glide path.

Origins

While most asset allocation plans call for a gradual reduction of risk taking as investors enter retirement and beyond, a couple of retirement experts—Wade Pfau of the American College of Financial Services and Michael Kitces, director of research at the Pinnacle Advisory Group—have come up with a new approach. Rather than entering retirement with around 50 percent or 60 percent in stocks and then, over a 30-year-plus retirement, dialing that down to 20 percent or even below, these experts support the reverse approach. As you enter retirement, drop your equity allocation down to an ultraconservative 30 percent or so. And then, as you progress through a decades-long retirement, gradually take on more risk and boost your stock weighting to as much as 50 percent or even higher.

In their recent paper, *Reducing Retirement Risk with a Rising Equity Glide-Path*, the two authors concluded,

> *We find, surprisingly, that rising equity glide-paths in retirement—where the portfolio starts out conservative and becomes more aggressive through the retirement time horizon—have the potential to actually reduce both the probability of failure and the magnitude of failure for client portfolios. This result may appear counter-intuitive from the traditional perspective, which is that equity exposure should decrease throughout retirement as the retiree's time horizon (and life expectancy) shrinks and mortality looms. Yet the conclusion is actually entirely logical when viewed from the perspective of what scenarios cause a client's retirement to "fail" in the first place.*

The Basics

Why does reversing the glide path at retirement seem to make sense, even when conventional wisdom says you should gradually dial down risk as your time horizon decreases? Simple. While your risk tolerance gradually lessens as you progress through life, the onset of actual retirement—at which point you no longer keep adding to your portfolio and instead begin the process of tapping the funds to pay for your basic needs—actually triggers another type of risk, on top of the market risk you already face. That's the risk of adding on to market losses.

For example, it's important to note that as a general rule of thumb, investors are warned not to withdraw money from their nest eggs too quickly. Historically, "too quickly" generally refers to tapping more than 4 percent of one's retirement funds in any given year. Go much higher than that—especially if you withdraw 6 percent or more of your account annually—and you run the risk of depleting your account well before you turn 90, which happens to be around the life expectancy of an individual who makes it to 65.

The trouble when it comes to retirement is if you happen to be the unlucky soul who quits work and starts tapping his or her retirement funds just as a bear market is set to begin. Think about how the combination of a bear market and your withdrawal patterns can devastate a nest egg at the onset of retirement. Say you retired in 2008, just before the market crash that saw equities lose nearly 40 percent of their value. And let's assume for the sake of argument that you retired with exactly $1 million in your nest egg, with plans to withdraw 4 percent of that, or $40,000, in the first year.

By the end of 2008, your original $1 million account would have shrunk to $600,000. And if you tapped an additional $40,000 on top of that to fund your living expenses, you'd end your first year if retirement with just $560,000. In other words, the combination of your withdrawals and the market loss has cut your entire nest egg almost in half—in just the first year. And if you were to keep withdrawing $40,000, which works out to a withdrawal rate of closer to 7 percent of the original sum, you'd be sure to run out of money before the end of your 30-year retirement.

This is why it's so important to be mindful of risk in the few years leading up to retirement and the first few years after retirement begins. The authors concluded,

> *In scenarios that threaten retirement sustainability—e.g., an extended period of poor returns in the first half of retirement—a declining equity exposure over time will lead the retiree to have the least in stocks if/when the good returns finally show up in the second half of retirement (assuming the entire retirement period does not experience continuing poor returns). With a rising equity glide path, the retiree is less exposed to losses when most vulnerable in early retirement and the equity exposure is greater by the time subsequent good returns finally show up. In turn, this helps to sustain greater retirement income over*

the entire time period. Conversely, using a rising equity glide-path in scenarios where equity returns are good early on, the retiree is so far ahead that their subsequent asset allocation choices do not impact the chances to achieve the original retirement goal.

The authors pointed out that over the course of a 30-year retirement, there's a 95 percent survival rate for a portfolio that begins with 30 percent stocks at retirement and gradually increases that exposure to 70 percent stocks in year 30 of retirement. This is again assuming a 4 percent withdrawal rate. If you flip that and start retirement at 70 percent equities, gradually working your way down to a 30 percent stock weighting by year 30, the odds of success fall to around 92 percent.

The Risk

Timing is everything. At the other end of the spectrum, think of what would have happened in another extreme period for the markets. Assume that you retired not in 2008, but in the 1990s, when stocks were routinely generating returns of more than 20 percent a year. Had you dropped your portfolio weighting to just 30 percent stocks in, say, 1995, you'd have missed out on the sizeable returns that stocks delivered, which helped retirees in that window of time bolster the strength of their nest eggs. Indeed, with rates of return that big, your retirement accounts would have grown substantially every year, even as you withdrew income from those funds. At average annual returns of 25 percent from 1995 through 1999, your nest egg would have grown substantially in the first five years of retirement even if you nudged the rules and withdrew twice as much as is recommended each year, or 8 percent.

That's just half of the picture. In addition to missing out on opportunities, you would have then taken that 30 percent weighting in stocks and gradually dialed up your risk to perhaps a 50 percent weighting in equities by the time the tech wreck came around in 2000, which would have cut your portfolio balance down by a significant amount. And if you stayed true to this approach and kept increasing your stock allocation for another several years, you might have held a majority of your post-retirement portfolio in equities just in time for the financial crisis in 2008 that led to yet another bear market.

Aside from the specific timing issue, there is another fundamental risk that you face with a rising glide path. While it's true that retirement can be a very long phase of life—and equities are often necessary for growth when investing over long stretches—many retirees face the real possibility of having unexpected healthcare costs hit them in the latter half of their retirement. By taking an increasingly aggressive stance toward investing in the latter half of retirement, you expose yourself. If a bear market strikes when you're in your late 70s or early 80s—and as much as 70 percent of your nest egg is in stocks—your retirement balances could suffer a massive blow just when you need that money to cover essential medical bills.

To be sure, not all retirees face these higher medical costs, and some have ample healthcare insurance to deal with the majority of those expenses. Still, you run the risk of having your plans upset by an unexpected emergency.

A Flat 60/40 Approach

The flat 60/40 approach is an old standard for asset allocation that can still be used today.

Origins

A classic 60 percent stock / 40 percent bond strategy is an old-fashioned approach to investing that simply balances the risks and rewards of stocks and bonds and gives a slight tilt toward equities. While viewed as a humdrum approach to investing, this boring strategy actually delivered nearly 90 percent of the returns of an all-stock portfolio since 1926—but with much less risk. The worst year for a 60 percent stock / 40 percent bond allocation, you'll recall, was a 26 percent decline for the S&P. While steep, that still pales in comparison to the 43 percent loss that a 100 percent U.S. stock portfolio suffered in 1931.

The Basics

The idea is simple. While many retirement advisers recommend that investors gradually reduce their exposure to equities over time, many still recommend that they keep as much as half or 60 percent of their nest eggs in equities to deliver growth for a retirement that could last more than 30 years. In fact, as you'll read in Chapter 9, many target date retirement funds, which are automated funds that take care of one's asset allocation decisions, hold around 60 percent of their assets in equities at retirement. Given that, some believe that there's nothing necessarily wrong with maintaining a reasonably flat exposure of 60 percent stocks and 40 percent bonds throughout one's life.

True, such a strategy would not take advantage of your additional ability to take on large amounts of risk early in your investing career. However, there are several advantages to this approach. First, it's the simplest plan to implement and stick to over time. As long as you rebalance your portfolio just once a year (see Chapter 8)—or choose a balanced mutual fund that will rebalance for you (more on that in Chapter 9)—you will always be on the right course, even if that glide path is not the most optimal approach for you at any particular stage of life.

Moreover, you never have to be prompted to change your allocation over time. That means there are no potential mistakes to be made on your part—for instance, forgetting to downshift your strategy at the proper time. Still another advantage is costs. Maintaining a 60 percent stock / 40 percent bond allocation requires only minor rebalancing from time to time (see Chapter 8). There is no wholesale need to sell stock and buy bonds in preparation for becoming more conservative over time. That, in turn, means that you are less likely to trigger capital gains taxes and trading costs with this simple approach. Similarly, there is no need to sell bonds and buy stocks if you choose to ramp up your aggressiveness once you get into retirement. There's also the fact that conventional wisdom is now at a crossroads. On the one hand, the traditionalists argue that you should enter retirement with a decent slug of stocks, at which point your investments should grow less conservative over time. Yet renegades like Pfau and Kitces argue that you should actually be less conservative at the start of retirement than you assume, and that your glide path should ascend over time once you are in retirement, not descend. Well, by sticking with a moderate 60 percent stock / 40 percent bond approach throughout retirement, you would actually be splitting the difference.

Finally, there is some evidence that would indicate that this strategy may not be overly simplistic after all. For starters, Vanguard ran some numbers and found that a basic 60 percent stock / 40 percent bond portfolio outperformed several sophisticated and well-known hedge fund strategies in the recent bear market from November 2007 to February 2009, as well as in the subsequent rally that took place from March 2009 to December 2011.

For example, the average performance of market neutral strategies (a common hedge fund technique that we will discuss later in this chapter) was a loss of 34 percent during the downturn, versus a decline of about 25 percent for the 60 percent stock / 40 percent bond portfolio. Yet in the subsequent rally that ran through December 2011, that same market neutral strategy—which investors pay up for—gained only around 4 percent, versus the 18 percent gain for the simple 60 percent stock / 40 percent bond approach.

Another common hedging strategy, known as long-short hedge funds, actually did beat the basic 60 percent stock / 40 percent bond approach in the 2007–2009 bear market. Long-short hedge funds lost around 17 percent during that stretch, or about 8 percentage points less than the simple 60/40 strategy. However, in the subsequent rebound, long-short funds also gained far less. The average long-short hedge fund returned just 7.5 percent between March 2009 and November 2011, which was more than 10 percentage points less than the 60/40 strategy produced.

More evidence in support of this 60/40 strategy can be found in the data that Pfau and Kitces assembled for their research on the effectiveness of a rising glide path strategy in retirement. Their research showed that starting in retirement at 30 percent stocks and dialing that up to 70 percent equities 30 years down the road gave your portfolio a 95 percent chance of success over a 30-year retirement, assuming you withdraw at a rate of 4 percent annually.

However, their same research showed that heading into retirement with a 60 percent weighting in stocks and remaining at 60 percent equities three decades later had a 93.2 percent chance of success—which wasn't that much worse than a rising glide path. Even more telling, this flat glide path led to an even greater chance of success than a traditional downward glide path strategy. For example, in this same example using the same assumptions, a retiree who starts off at 65 with 60 percent in stocks and ratchets that down to 10 percent by age 95 has a 92.8 percent chance of maintaining an account balance over a 30-year retirement, assuming a 4 percent withdrawal rate. If that retiree starts at that same 60 percent equity stake and takes an even more risk-averse downward glide path—with zero percent in stocks at the end of retirement—the odds of success are even lower: 92.4 percent.

The Risk

There are a couple of big risks to be aware of with a strategy that does not call for dialing down risk as you grow older. One is the risk of being unlucky enough to retire amid—or just before the start of—a bear market in equities that can drastically reduce the value and longevity of your retirement account. Remember, had you begun retirement in 2008 with $1 million invested in a 60 percent stock / 40 percent bond strategy, you'd have ended the year down by about $200,000.

Then you would have needed to withdraw income from that depleted account, reducing the balance even more. Even at a conservative 4 percent withdrawal rate, that would amount to reducing your account value by another $40,000 or so. This means that by sticking with a stock-heavy mix at the onset of retirement, you would have immediately depleted nearly one-quarter of your portfolio in year one in this example. This would have drastically reduced your odds of being able to live a comfortable life in retirement as planned.

The second concern is more specific to the era we seem to be entering into. The historic annual return for bonds has been around 6 percent since 1926. Meanwhile, equities have delivered returns of about 10 percent annually from that same date. This implies that a balanced 60 percent stock / 40 percent bond strategy should return around 8.8 percent a year over the long course of time, which is pretty substantial.

However, you have to keep in mind that just because a certain asset allocation strategy returns a set amount over the long term, doesn't necessarily mean that it will deliver the same level of returns in the short or near term. In fact, based on the valuations of both the stock and bond markets, many market strategists predict that we could be in store for a prolonged period of subpar gains, which would make a 60 percent stock / 40 percent bond portfolio less than appealing.

Take bonds. When it comes to government bonds, a classic way to gauge how well they are expected to perform, from a total return standpoint, going forward is to consider what 10-year Treasury bonds are yielding today. The investment management firm Leuthold Group studied this relationship between future bond returns and current yields and found the correlation between the two to be surprisingly strong. So, for instance, in January 1970, 10-year Treasury notes were yielding about 7 percent. Throughout the following decade, government bonds returned about 7 percent annually, according to Ibbotson. Similarly, in January 1990, 10-year bonds were yielding around 8 percent, and sure enough, government bonds wound up delivering average annual returns of around 8 percent for the next decade.

Today, the 10-year yield stands at around 2.5 percent, which means that there's a strong likelihood that over the next decade, your government bonds will deliver returns of just 2.5 percent a year, or less than half their historic gains.

Similarly, there is a simple—and historically accurate—tool to predict future stock market returns. It starts by taking the price/earnings ratio for equities. But not just any P/E ratio—the idea is to take the "normalized" or averaged profits for the market over several years. The Leuthold Group prefers to use five years, and based on that measure, the S&P 500 was trading at a normalized P/E of 22 in late 2013. Now, divide 1 by that P/E (the inverse of a stock's P/E ratio is called its earnings yield). So 1 divided by 22 equals 0.045, or 4.5 percent.

This figure is a back-of-the-envelope forecast for annual stock returns over the next decade. Now combine the two. With a 60 percent weighting in equities and a 40 percent stake in bonds, a balanced portfolio going forward is likely to return around 3.7 percent. Even if you round that up to 4 percent annual returns, that would work out to less than half the gains that this strategy has historically generated. So while a flat 60 percent stock / 40 percent bond approach may seem appropriate, there are no guarantees that it can provide the growth going forward that it has in the past.

Alternative Assets

In addition to alternative theories that have become part of today's asset allocation conversation, there are several investments that are beginning to work their way into the discussion of just what an alternative asset truly is.

Historically, the term *alternative asset* has been reserved for a couple of larger categories of investments that go beyond stocks and bonds. They include commodities (ranging from precious metals such as gold and silver to industrial metals such as steel, aluminum, and copper to agricultural commodities such as wheat, corn and cotton) and real estate (whether held as physical properties for appreciation or to generate rental income, or through investment vehicles such as real estate investment trusts). Both of these types of alternative assets were used to hedge specific risks in the market, such as the risk of rising prices and inflation, which hard assets such as real estate and commodities are good at shielding against.

The investments described in this section still have a long way to go before they are included in the basic canon of alternatives such as commodities and real estate. And some, in fact, represent subasset classes rather than stand-alone categories of investments. But they are growing in use and in popularity, and they are being discussed as vehicles to help investors reach certain goals—for instance, seeking growth, income, and hedging their bets.

For Growth

Alternative assets that can be used to seek growth include micro-cap stocks and frontier market stocks.

Micro-Cap Stocks
What are they?

In the universe of stocks, there are mega caps (the largest of the large-cap stocks), large-cap shares, an in-between category known as mid-cap stocks (which are medium-sized companies that are growing slightly faster than large caps but that are more stable, in general, than small caps), small-cap companies, and finally the micro caps.

Whereas the typical small-company stock might have a market value of around $500 million or higher, a micro-capitalization stock is a publicly traded company whose stock market value is even smaller than that—often between $50 million and $300 million (Table 7-1).

TABLE 7–1 Market Caps *Typical market value of companies based on "cap" size.*	
Stock Type	**Market Capitalization (Value)**
Mega Cap	Over $50 billion
Large Cap	Over $10 billion
Mid Cap	$3 billion to $10 billion
Small Cap	$500 million to $3 billion
Micro Cap	$50 million to $500 million

Why bet on such small, risky companies? Well, if the idea behind investing in small stocks is to find the next Google or Microsoft—before they get discovered by other investors—you're more apt to be first if you look at really tiny enterprises. Moreover, you're more apt to make really big money by identifying the "next big things" before they get big, when these companies are in their infancy, not when they are toddlers. Or so the theory goes. Obviously, it is much more difficult to spot the next generation of leading companies at such an early stage. But one thing going for you is lack of competition.

A typical large-cap company is followed by dozens of Wall Street analysts whose job it is to track small trends in a company's business and business model that will give their clients—investors—a competitive edge. With so many analysts looking for the same thing, there actually ceases to be a competitive edge, which is why it's so hard to beat the market by picking large blue chip stocks.

Part of the small-cap advantage all along has been that fewer analysts are apt to follow these companies, giving individual investors an opportunity to spot surprises and to exploit them for gains. Well, when it comes to micro-cap stocks, that advantage is all the more amplified. Whereas a small publicly traded company might have three to five analysts tracking it on a day-to-day basis, many micro-cap stocks have one or fewer analysts covering them. This leads to greater risks, of course, since this means that micro-cap stocks are more prone to surprising Wall Street. On the other hand, those surprises are just the type of opportunities that investors require to beat the performance of the broad market.

Risks and shortcomings

The obvious risk with micro caps is that these are smaller businesses that are much more prone to out-and-out failure than large-cap companies. By definition, a micro-cap stock is less well financed than a blue chip firm is. And unless it has a breakthrough technology that literally creates a new market for growth, a micro-cap company will often be a tiny player in markets that are likely to be dominated by big, globally oriented companies with deeper pockets and influence.

This vulnerability also makes micro-cap stocks much more volatile than large stocks. Over the past five years, the standard deviation of the iShares Micro-Cap stock index fund has been 23, which makes these stocks around 10 percent riskier than small-cap stocks and 40 percent riskier than large-cap shares (Table 7-2).

Higher volatility means that as the broad stock market ebbs and flows, the highs are likely to be higher with micro caps than with small caps and especially with large caps. On the other hand, the lows are likely to be even lower. Indeed, in 2008, when small stocks lost around 37 percent of their value amid the global financial crisis, micro-cap stocks lost closer to 40 percent.

Frontier Market Stocks
What are they?

You know what an emerging market stock is—shares of companies based in developing economies that are just starting to accelerate, such as China, India, Russia,

TABLE 7–2 Size Versus Volatility
Historically, the smaller a stock is, the more rocky its ride.

Market Cap	Standard Deviation Past 5 Years
Mega Cap	16.0
Large Cap	16.3
Mid Cap	18.7
Small Cap	21.9
Micro Cap	23.1

Source: Morningstar

and Latin America. Well, frontier market stocks are shares of companies based in even less-developed parts of the world.

In Africa, that includes countries like Nigeria, Tunisia, and Kenya. In Asia, this includes Vietnam, Sri Lanka, Pakistan, and Bangladesh. In Eastern Europe, this includes really nascent economies such as Croatia, Estonia, and Lithuania. The frontier markets also include large swaths of the Middle East, including markets such as Bahrain, Oman, Kuwait, Qatar, and the United Arab Emirates.

While some investors regard frontier market stocks as a subset of the larger emerging market category, others break it out into its own grouping. Why? For one thing, frontier markets tend to look slightly different from many of the more established emerging markets. While maturing emerging market economies like China and India are coveted for their industrial strength and the consumers in their burgeoning middle class, frontier market are still largely a play on natural resources and raw materials. Oil-rich countries in the Middle East, in fact, make up more than half of some frontier market indexes.

There's another reason why some investors have started to break out frontier markets into their own category. While emerging markets are still growing faster than the developed world, the rapid maturation of these economies in recent years has begun to slow that growth. Corporate profits in the emerging markets, for example, are expected to grow around 12 percent to 13 percent a year for the next five years or so. That's certainly faster than the 8 percent to 10 percent growth lately for the S&P 500. But it's still much slower than the 18 percent growth seen in the frontier markets.

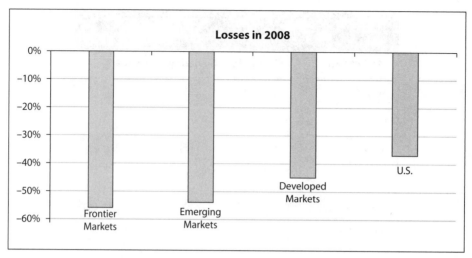

FIGURE 7–1 Frontier Risks

Frontier market earnings are growing faster than average, but these stocks can also lose ground faster than average.

Source: MSCI

Risks and shortcomings

The emerging markets are risky enough given the political risks and currency fluctuations you face when investing in still-developing nations. Those risks are all the more amplified when it comes to the frontier markets, which are dominated by exposure to oil-rich Africa and the Middle East. Indeed, more than 80 percent of the iShares MSCI Frontier 100 ETF is held in companies based just in Africa and the Middle East. Any geopolitical crisis that affects those regions is likely to impact those stocks, even if the companies you own aren't directly associated with the energy markets.

Also, bear in mind that many of the companies that are based in the frontier markets are also just starting to grow. This is why the average holding in a frontier market fund or exchange-traded fund tends to be much smaller than the average holding in a typical U.S. blue chip stock fund. In fact, the average stock in the iShares MSCI Frontier 100 ETF is just $5 billion, making it more of a mid-cap stock than a blue chip. This simply adds to the additional volatility you're likely to experience when owning frontier stocks.

Given these risks, and given that emerging market stocks are generally limited to around 10 percent of your equity stake, it's wise to limit your frontier market stake even more.

For Income

An alternative asset that can be used for income is fixed immediate annuities.

Fixed Immediate Annuities
What are they?

A fixed immediate annuity isn't actually an investment per se. It's an insurance contract that you buy with a lump sum of money. In return, the insurance company promises to deliver to you a set amount of monthly income for the rest of your life—even if you live well beyond the life expectancy of 90.

An immediate annuity is not to be confused with a variable annuity, which is a tax-sheltered vehicle with an insurance wrapper that allows you to invest money in stock funds and bond funds in a tax-advantaged manner during your working years. While a variable annuity is similar to a 401(k) account that comes with an element of insurance, a fixed immediate annuity is like a personal pension that you can buy with cash. The insurance company commits to pay you a level of monthly income based on your age, health, and gender, along with market interest rates. And it's the insurance company—not you—that assumes the investment risk to be able to make such payouts over the course of possibly three decades or longer.

If it's not an investment, how does a fixed immediate annuity qualify as a budding alternative asset? Because of the role an immediate annuity can play in a diversified portfolio at, and into, retirement. At retirement, for example, investors are conventionally advised to increase their bond allocations. And as they begin to tap their accounts to fund their retirement needs, they are advised to withdraw no more than 4 percent annually from their accounts.

Even in the recent low-interest-rate environment, many fixed annuities were paying out more than what a 4 percent withdrawal rate could. For example, in 2013, a 65-year-old man who purchased a $100,000 annuity could expect around $550 in monthly income, or around $6,600 a year. By comparison, if you were to take that same $100,000 and put it into bonds, you could expect only $4,000 a year in safe annual withdrawals using the 4 percent rule.

How can insurance companies promise you the safe delivery of what is in essence a 6 percent withdrawal rate, guaranteed, over an entire retirement without fear of depleting those account balances prematurely? Simple: Insurance companies can do something no individual can—they can spread out the risk of longevity over a large pool of other annuity investors. So while you might live well beyond your expected life expectancy, other annuity buyers may pass away earlier than expected. The cash that they leave on the table as a result of their premature passing—and that would have otherwise gone to issuing them guaranteed checks for years to come—can then be used toward the investment needs of the remaining lives in the pool.

An annuity is a contract, but any contract is only as strong as the company that makes that promise. So when you buy an annuity, you should look for a large, financially healthy insurer with a AAA rating. With that in place, you can consider an immediate annuity similar to an investment in a bond. So, for instance, say you have a $500,000 nest egg and feel comfortable investing that in a 50 percent stock / 50 percent bond allocation. Now let's assume that at retirement, you carve out $200,000 of that money and use it to buy a fixed immediate annuity. Now you could invest the remaining $300,000 in a 50 percent stock / 50 percent bond mix. However, you must remember that the annuity you just purchased is bondlike. Given that, you can afford to take additional risks with the remaining $300,000, since $200,000 is already in a bondlike instrument. So, depending on your preference, you might choose to invest $200,000 of the remaining cash in stocks and $100,000 in bonds.

Risks and shortcomings

There are a couple of big concerns when it comes to buying a fixed immediate annuity. The first is that the insurer that you sign the contract with could run into financial problems that would force it to default on its obligation.

You can mitigate this risk if you go with the highest financially rated insurers. And as with any other investment, you can reduce company-specific risks through diversification. For instance, there is no rule that says that you must buy a single annuity through just one insurer. In fact, it probably doesn't make any sense to. If you want to annuitize, say, $250,000, you can split that amount into two separate contracts with two different financial companies to protect against the possibility that one of those firms will run into financial difficulties. Or you can could even divide that sum five ways and select five different insurers through which to invest $50,000 each. That way, should any single annuity provider go out of business, the other four would still be able to provide you with income.

And even in the event that an annuity provider goes bust, your funds may not necessarily be entirely lost. In the event of a company failure, state insurance regulators will step in and liquidate assets to help fulfill the financial obligations of the company. There are also state-run reserve funds that help serve as a backstop should policyholders need protection.

The other risk comes with having to hand over a lump sum of what could be tens if not hundreds of thousands of dollars at retirement—and not having access to that cash to meet other needs. For example, as was stated earlier, a common concern for older retirees is a medical emergency or the onset of a chronic medical condition that could lead to unexpected big healthcare bills. If you were to hand over a quarter or a third or more of your nest egg early on in retirement, you could be cutting off access to the one source of funds you have to meet those potential bills. Without access to that cash, you may be forced to sell other investments that are more liquid even if that means upsetting your entire asset allocation plan.

For Hedging

Two alternative assets that can be used for hedging are inverse funds and market neutral funds.

Inverse Funds
What are they?

An inverse fund is one that promises to deliver the results of a particular market—only in the opposite direction. Sometimes referred to as bear funds, these portfolios use options contracts and other derivative investments to do the inverse of what the broad market does. So on a day in which the S&P 500 might rise 1 percent, you can expect an S&P 500 bear fund to fall 1 percent. Conversely, on a day when the S&P 500 falls 1 percent, the inverse version is expected to rise about 1 percent.

There are inverse mutual funds and ETFs that hedge your exposure to broad market indexes such as the S&P 500, the Nasdaq 100 index, or the Russell 2000 index of small stocks. There are even inverse funds that let you bet against stock markets in specific regions, such as Europe, Latin America, and Japan.

There are even variations of the bear market fund that, through the addition of leverage, even promise to deliver twice the inverse results of any particular market. So if the Russell 2000 small stock index were to fall 2 percent on a given day, you would expect the ProFunds UltraShort Small-Cap fund to gain 4 percent.

How can these funds be used in your portfolio? Well, if you think that we're in for a long stretch of market losses—within a bear market or a correction, for instance—the idea would be to use these funds to make money even as stock prices are falling. Even if you were pessimistic about the direction of the markets, it would be extraordinarily risky to shift your entire equity portfolio into such a fund. However, by taking a small percentage of your holdings—say, less than 10 percent—and investing in such an inverse fund, you would ensure that not all parts of your equity portfolio would fall should the market collapse, as it did in 2008.

The idea of betting against the market can be risky, but these funds purport to be a safer way to do that than through the traditional method of using margin accounts to "short" stocks. In the traditional strategy of short selling, you would typically borrow shares of a stock that you don't own from your broker's inventory, with the idea of selling those borrowed shares and getting credited with that sales price. Then, at a later date, after the stock price falls, you would buy the actual shares at the new lower price and return them to your broker/lender while pocketing the difference. Sounds great, but if the price of the stock goes up instead of down, you will lose money on the transaction. And if the stock price rises too much and too quickly, your broker may demand that you cover the cost of the borrowed shares, which may force you to sell other holdings in your portfolio prematurely if you don't have the cash.

An inverse fund avoids these concerns because you are not taking out a margin account through which to borrow any shares. You are simply putting the money to work in a fund whose value will fluctuate with the market in an inverse manner.

Risks and shortcomings

There are a couple of big risks when it comes to using inverse funds. The first is that you are betting against market history.

Over long periods of time, stocks are apt to rise in value more than twice as often as they are to fall on any given day. So over the course of any given week, you are more likely to suffer losses in an inverse fund than receive gains—and big losses if you use a leveraged fund that promises twice the inverse results of any given market.

It's not just over the short term. Over the long run, the S&P 500 has posted positive gains in 61 out of the past 85 calendar years, in 70 out of the past 81 rolling 5-year stretches, in 72 out of the past 76 rolling 10-year periods; and in all 66 of the past rolling 20-year stretches, according to Ibbotson. As a result, the odds are against you if you plan to use these funds as a permanent holding in your asset allocation strategy (Figure 7-2).

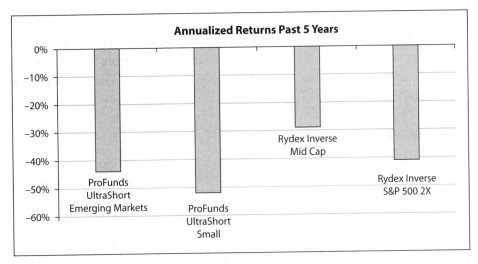

FIGURE 7–2 Inverse Risks

There is a major risk in holding an inverse fund as a permanent holding.

Source: Morningstar

Another thing to consider is the fact that while these funds try to deliver the inverse results of the market on any given day, over really long periods of time, they cannot precisely replicate the opposite results of any broad market. That's because over time, returns are compounded in an uneven fashion due to the leverage effect and the random order of returns. For example, even in the worst of all downturns, stocks will not lose money on every single day. Nor will they lose money in a straight line. As a result, if there are enough up days in a down market, these funds may not deliver twice as much as the market loses in any bear market stretch. In fact, they aren't even guaranteed to make you money, period, in a stretch where the market is down. Take, for example, the disappointing five-year stretch between March 2000 and March 2005, when the S&P 500 lost approximately 5 percent of its value. You would think that an inverse fund that promises to deliver two times the opposite results of the S&P 500 would have gained around 10 percent during this stretch. Instead, the ProFunds UltraBear fund actually lost 17 percent of its value.

How come? Well, this was not a singularly bad period for stocks. This five-year window of time encompassed the bear market that ran from March 2000 to October 2002. But it also captured parts of the bull market that began in late 2002 and ran for the next five years. The combination of bull and bear days, in addition to the up days within the 2000–2002 bear market, wound up twisting the results in an unexpected fashion.

It's not just this one period. Over the past decade through November 2013, U.S. stocks delivered gains of around 7.8 percent. So the expectation is that a two-times inverse S&P 500 fund should be down around 15 percent. Nope, instead, the ProFunds UltraBear fund lost considerably more: it was down 22 percent a year during this same 10-year period.

Market Neutral Funds
What are they?

The name sure sounds appealing. A market neutral fund is a hedge fund–like investment that attempts to deliver positive results regardless of what type of market conditions exist. These funds use a combination of techniques—including derivatives, shorting, and in some cases leverage—to engineer positive results in both good markets and bad. Who wouldn't want to own a stock fund that can rise even if the broad market is falling?

Many of these fund fall under the general category of "long-short" funds, which give managers license to simultaneously bet on stocks (as you would do in any traditional fund) while also betting against other shares. The idea is create a port-folio whose performance has almost nothing to do with the general direction of the market.

The appeal is apparent: if you can find a way to make money in any market environment, then you reduce the volatility in your portfolio while also ensuring certainty and predictability in your results.

Risks and shortcomings

It may sound like a perfectly reasonable idea to let managers go long on stocks they are confident in while shorting others that they feel will fall. There's an inherent risk in that, though: What if the manager is wrong on both calls? Such a long-short approach may take some of the market risks out of the equation. However, this strategy could just as easily amplify another risk: the risk that your fund manager is flawed.

There are other risks with this approach too. For starters, there are no guaran-tees that these funds will always post positive returns in up or down markets. In fact, the average market neutral fund has lost value (though by slight amounts) in four of the past six years.

And as with all hedging techniques, you have to give up something. In this case, while a market neutral fund can be downright appealing in down markets, it can be less advantageous in up markets, since the hedging techniques it employs will likely weigh down its potential returns in a bull market. Indeed, in 2008, the average market neutral fund was essentially flat, posting average losses of just 0.3 percent at a time when the average stock fund fell 37 percent. But in the subsequent year—2009, when the S&P 500 soared more than 26 percent—market neutral funds lost 1.2 percent. The year after that, when stocks rose 15 percent, the average market neutral fund lost again—falling 2 percent. And the year after that, when the S&P 500 posted gains of 2 percent, market neutral funds lost again, falling 0.3 percent.

All in all, over the past decade, the average market neutral fund has gained only 2 percent, which means that you would have done far better by hedging your equity risk through good old-fashioned bonds.

QUIZ

1. The leveraged life-cycle strategy calls for what level of equity exposure in your 20s?
   A. 50 percent
   B. 100 percent
   C. 150 percent
   D. 200 percent

2. Using leverage early on will allow you to take on which of the following closer to retirement?
   A. More risk
   B. Less risk
   C. The same risk

3. Under the leveraged life-cycle approach, you are supposed to leverage which of the following asset classes?
   A. Just stocks
   B. Just bonds
   C. Stocks and bonds
   D. All your assets

4. Under the rising glide path theory, which of the following allocations are supposed to climb?
   A. Stocks
   B. Bonds
   C. Stocks and bonds
   D. Neither

5. The rising glide path theory calls for increasing your risk taking at which stage of life?
   A. In your 20s and 30s, when you have greater tolerance for risk
   B. In your 40s, when your income is growing
   C. Just prior to retirement
   D. Just after retirement

6. **What is a good target equity allocation at retirement under the rising glide path theory?**
   A. 30 percent
   B. 50 percent
   C. 60 percent
   D. 70 percent

7. **In your 30s, what is likely to be your single biggest asset?**
   A. Stocks
   B. Bonds
   C. Your income
   D. Cash

8. **In your 30s, what ought to be your single biggest investable asset?**
   A. Stocks
   B. Bonds
   C. Your income
   D. Cash

9. **Buying a fixed immediate annuity at retirement allows you to be …**
   A. Less aggressive with your asset allocation.
   B. More aggressive with your asset allocation.
   C. Risk averse in retirement.

10. **Market neutral funds are designed to take which risk out of the equation?**
    A. Market risk
    B. Manager risk
    C. Timing risk
    D. Interest rate risk

chapter **8**

Establishing a Rebalancing Strategy

Any asset allocation strategy that you implement, no matter how sound and effective the approach, won't be complete if you don't establish a rebalancing strategy to go along with it. *Rebalancing* refers to the simple act of routinely resetting your mix of stocks, bonds, and other asset classes back to their intended mix.

One way to achieve this is by directing new money into assets that have fallen in value to replenish your overall allocations. But the most common approach to this strategy is to sell some of your winning investments and use that money to replenish your exposure to underperforming asset classes.

This may seem counterintuitive to you, since you've probably been taught that "buy and hold"—that is, being patient and letting your investments grow untouched over time—is a prudent approach to take. And it is. But buy and hold pertains to how you treat your individual stocks and funds. Once you purchase an individual security, you should have the patience and discipline to let it gradually appreciate in value. But when it comes to managing your overall collection of assets—i.e., your total weighting in stocks versus bonds versus other assets—you have to be willing to make periodic adjustments *in order* to stay the course.

Think of yourself as a gardener. After planting the seeds of your asset allocation strategy, you must tend it like a growing garden every now and then. Why? Because like a garden, your portfolio's exposure to various asset classes will grow and change over time. The only thing is, they won't all grow at the same pace. Stocks will likely outpace bonds and cash over the long run. There are plenty of years, though, in which your bonds will outperform stocks and other investments. Before you know it, the strategy that you implement will turn into something quite unfamiliar, and your goal is to prevent that from happening.

If You Don't Rebalance, the Market Will Rebalance for You

Here's a classic example of the situation you're trying to avoid: Say it's the year 1994, and you decide that the best allocation strategy for you is to have 60 percent of your money in equities and 40 percent in bonds. Over the subsequent five years, between 1995 and 1999, the S&P 500 index of blue chip stocks, fueled by a technology boom that evolved into the Internet mania, went on to post an astounding 29 percent annual average return, something virtually unheard of prior to that period. At the same time, U.S. bonds delivered pretty much what you would expect, based on historic norms: average annual returns of around 5.7 percent.

As a stock investor, the outsized gains in the late 1990s would have made you ecstatic. After all, had you put $60,000 into equities that year, your stock portfolio would have more than tripled in value, to an astounding $210,500. Is there anything wrong with that? Well, by 1999, the fact that your stocks were growing at five times the pace of your bonds meant that your original moderate, play-it-safe 60 percent stock / 40 percent bond strategy would have morphed into an *80 percent stock / 20 percent bond* portfolio. That means you went from a modest-risk portfolio to an aggressive-risk strategy. Moreover, you went from a modest-income portfolio to a low-income portfolio (Figure 8-1).

Worse still is the timing of this move (or lack thereof). Being an aggressive investor at the end of 1999—just before the bursting of the tech bubble and one of the worst bear markets in history—proved to be devastating to many investors, especially those who were nearing retirement. A person who was in the final years of his or her working career with $1 million on March 2000, at the start of the tech bubble bear market, would have seen his or her nest egg shrink to $724,000 by the end of 2002, on the brink of heading into retirement. Had that same person rebalanced prior to the bear market, thereby reducing the exposure to equities back to 60 percent on a routine basis, the investor still would have lost money, but he or she would have lost around $100,000 less.

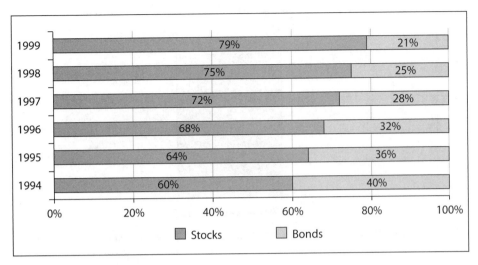

FIGURE 8–1 How Allocations Shift
If you don't rebalance, the market will change your allocation for you.

Okay, but wasn't this a rare occurrence? Isn't this an overly extreme example that might not affect too many people in reality? Sadly, no. Just five years after the end of the 2000–2002 bear market, investors ran headlong into an even more severe crash in late 2007 and 2008, stemming from the onset of the global financial panic caused by the housing downturn and the meltdown in the market for mortgage-related debt. Whereas the 2000–2002 bear market erased nearly half the total value of U.S. stocks, the downturn that ran from October 2007 to March 2009 eradicated nearly 60 cents of every dollar that investors had in the market.

A study by the Employee Benefit Research Institute, which periodically tracks the state of retirement readiness and confidence, found that heading into the financial crisis, 22 percent of all participants in 401(k) retirement plans (where the government gives you a tax break for saving for your golden years, but where you assume all the investment risks and make all the investment decisions) who were 56 to 65 years old (meaning they were either at or less than 10 years from retirement) held an astounding 90 percent of their nest eggs in stocks, with 10 percent or less in fixed income (Figure 8-2).

In other words, by failing to rebalance, those workers who most needed to protect their assets because of their shortened time horizon were investing more aggressively than is advised even for their kids or grandchildren. A $1 million 90 percent stock / 10 percent bond portfolio at the start of the bear market in

FIGURE 8–2 Older Workers and Stocks

In 2007, before the financial crisis, many older boomers held a dangerous amount in equities in their 401(k)s.

Source: EBRI

October 2007 would have shrunk to a mere $497,000 by the downturn's end in 2009.

The situation was actually more widespread than that. While one out of five older baby boomers who were nearing retirement held 90 percent of their 401(k)s in stocks, one out of three held 80 percent or more of their retirement accounts in equities. And nearly one in two older workers held 70 percent or more of their retirement funds in stocks.

Some got to this overly aggressive stance by choice—equities had been in a bull market from September 2002 to October 2007, and some investors simply found it too difficult to sell an investment that was making so much money at the time for fear that they'd miss out on future gains. Other investors, though, got there by neglect. Surveys of 401(k) investors routinely find that the vast majority—in some cases, 80 percent or more—of retirement investors go several years without touching their 401(k)s, whether to buy a new fund or simply reallocate.

Regardless, by failing to routinely prune your equity position during those times when your investments are climbing in value, a comfortable retirement could easily turn into a truncated one. Or more likely a delayed one, as many workers had to go back to the workforce to replenish their nest eggs.

Understand the Math of Recovery

Even the 50-somethings in this example, who had the most time among older workers to recover from such a severe bear market, faced a daunting road to recovery, which is another reason why rebalancing is so important.

Here's a simple illustration: Say you had $1 million invested in stocks at the start of the downturn, and by the end you were left with closer to $400,000. How long do you think it would take to get back to even? Well, if history is any guide, it could take years. For instance, if equities deliver their historic average annual returns of around 10 percent, it would take a full 10 years for a $400,000 stock portfolio to get back to the $1 million mark. This means that a decade later, you'd still be only where you were at the start. Why does it take so long to rebound?

You have to understand how the market's math works. Many investors incorrectly assume that a 50 percent decline in an investment simply requires a 50 percent gain to come back to even. Unfortunately, that's not the way gains and losses work. A 50 percent drop in stock value, for example, would require that your investment rebound by 100 percent just to get back to the starting level. (After all, a 50 percent decline from a $100 investment would leave you with $50. But from those lows, you'd require a $50 gain to get you back to $100, which is doubling your original amount at the market's low.)

The rule of thumb is, the more you lose, the greater the gains required to break even—and the greater the disparity between your original loss and the gains required to recover. For example, if your portfolio were simply to fall 5 percent, going from $100,000 in value to $95,000, getting back to the $100,000 level would require you to make 5.3 percent in the rebound. Lose 10 percent, and you'd have to make 11.1 percent. If you suffer a 20 percent drop, your investments would have to earn 25 percent to make you whole again. But at 50 percent, it jumps to 100 percent (Table 8-1).

The moral of this story is that by keeping your losses modest by establishing an appropriate asset allocation plan—and then making sure that your strategy remains appropriate for you by rebalancing periodically—you will ensure that you won't suffer losses so severe that it could take you years, if not decades, to recover.

TABLE 8–1 Losing Math *The bigger the loss, even bigger the gains needed to fully recover.*	
If you lost this amount...	**...You'd have to earn this to get back to even**
–5%	+5.3%
–10%	+11.1%
–20%	+25%
–30%	+43%
–40%	+66.7%
–50%	+100%
–60%	+150%

Appreciate the Odds of Losing

Okay, but the 2000s were an anomaly, right? How many "lost decades" does the market suffer? Well, since the Great Depression began in 1929, there have been eight full decades of market history. And four of those eight decades—the 1930s, 1940s, 1970s, and 2000s—were considered troubled or lost stretches (Table 8-2). So the odds of running into an extraordinarily difficult stretch for stocks seem close to 50-50. Still, this isn't the right question to be asking.

The better question that investors must ask is this: How frequently are you likely to run into any setback or downturn in the market? The answer is more frequently than you might assume. Putnam Research went back and studied all the past bull and bear markets that have occurred since 1948. What the asset management firm discovered was that over this 65-year stretch, there have been 13 official bear markets, defined by at least a 20 percent decline in stock values (Table 8-3). And each bear market lasted about 14 months. This means that your odds of running into a market correction—in which failing to rebalance will hurt you—is about roughly one out of every five years.

TABLE 8–2 Taking Stock of Decades
How equities performed, on an inflation-adjusted basis, in past decades.

Year	Real Stock Gains
2000s	–3.4%
1990s	15.3%
1980s	12.5%
1970s	–1.5%
1960s	5.3%
1950s	17.2
1940s	3.8
1930s	1.9%

Source: Ibbotson Associates

TABLE 8–3 Bear Markets
A list of all bear markets in U.S. stocks since World War II.

Dates	Market Loss
10/9/2007 to 3/9/2009	–57%
3/24/2000 to 10/9/2002	–49%
7/16/1990 to 10/11/1990	–20%
8/25/1987 to 12/4/1987	–34%
11/28/1980 to 8/12/1982	–27%
1/11/1973 to 10/3/1974	–48%
11/29/1968 to 5/26/1970	–36%
2/9/1966 to 10/7/1966	–22%
12/12/1961 to 6/27/1962	–28%
8/2/1956 to 10/22/1957	–22%
5/29/1946 to 6/13/1949	–30%

Source: S&P

Beware of Being Whipsawed

The risks of failing to rebalance don't stop with the losses you suffer in a down-turn. While it's bad enough to suffer worse-than-expected losses because you are overweight in a particular asset class at the worst possible moment, there's the flip side to think about.

And that is, at the end of every market correction, there is an eventual rebound. And failing to rebalance—in this case, by being courageous enough to replenish your stake in a falling asset, rather than simply paring your exposure to a rising investment—not only means that your losses in the downturn will be worse than expected, it also means there's a good chance that your gains in the subsequent recovery will also be less than desired.

Case in point: Say you began 2000 with a 60 percent stock / 40 percent bond portfolio, and then the bear market struck. For three straight years, the S&P 500 sank precipitously (falling 9.1 percent, 11.9 percent, and then 22.1 percent), reducing your equity exposure along the way. During the downturn, if you had not periodically rebalanced by buying stocks to get you back to the 60 percent exposure, you'd have ended up with just a 40 percent weighting in stocks in 2003. This would have happened at the beginning of a rewarding bull market that lasted for five years. In this case, by failing to rebalance back into stocks, you ended up with less exposure to this asset class than a retiree would have had. So as you can see, rebalancing works in both directions.

The Purpose of Rebalancing

Rebalancing serves three important purposes: to maintain an appropriate level of risk, to ensure that you routinely take some profits, and to make sure that you always sell high and buy low.

1. To Maintain an Appropriate Level of Risk, Not to Squeeze Out Extra Gains.

There are plenty of academic studies that show that refusing to rebalance actually leads to better performance over the very long term. And there's some logic to that. If stocks historically outperform bonds and other assets, it stands to reason that if you refuse to rebalance, your equity exposure will eventually rise over time.

And that in turn means that your portfolio ought to deliver you greater returns than if you had rebalanced along the way.

In fact, the Vanguard Group studied the performance of a 60 percent stock / 40 percent bond strategy that was launched in 1926. Researchers there found that by 2009, that original 60/40 strategy would have netted you an annualized return of 9.1 percent (Figure 8-3). That's roughly half a percentage point more than a routinely rebalanced 60/40 portfolio would have yielded during that same stretch of time. Over time, that makes for a big difference in performance. Invest $100,000 for 25 years at 9.1 percent interest, and you'll wind up with $882,000. Invest that same amount for the same time at annual returns of 8.5 percent, and you'd arrive at $768,000—or $114,000 less.

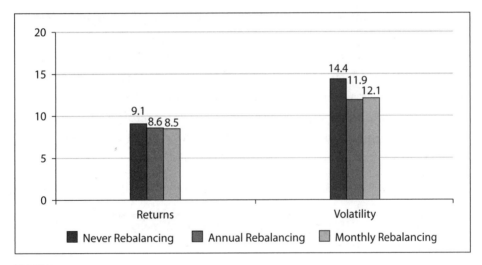

FIGURE 8–3 The Pros and Cons of Rebalancing
Never rebalancing can add returns—and risk—to your portfolio.
Since 1926. *Source:* Vanguard

Of course, there is no such thing as a free lunch when it comes to investing. So what price do you pay for that extra return? That same Vanguard study found that in exchange for obtaining that extra half a percent of gains a year over time, you expose your portfolio to nearly 20 percent greater volatility by not rebalancing than if you had readjusted your portfolio periodically. The question that you have to ask yourself is, are you willing to lose—or, more to the point, financially capable of losing—20 percent more than the stock market during major downturns in exchange for that extra incremental gain?

The Great Debate

Can rebalancing actually make you more money over time? Some proponents of rebalancing will actually make this argument. And you can find evidence for rebalancing leading to higher gains—if you cherry-pick the perfect time periods to make that case. Here's a classic example. Researchers at T. Rowe Price, the mutual fund company, examined how a basic $100,000 portfolio comprised of 60 percent stocks, 30 percent bonds, and 10 percent cash would have performed over time based on various rebalancing strategies.

What they found was that if this portfolio were never rebalanced, it would have grown to $630,100 by September 2002. By comparison, a portfolio that was rebalanced once a year would have left you with $634,700 by that same date. Great. But that's in part because the end date of that analysis coincided with one of the worst bear markets in history, which adversely affected the more aggressive non-rebalancing approach.

The T. Rowe Price researchers noted that if you extended the time frame out four more years, ending in a bull market (and conveniently missing the 2007–2009 bear market that wreaked havoc on stock-heavy portfolios), the results would have looked very different. In that case, the ending value of the rebalanced portfolio was $925,200, versus $1 million for the non-rebalanced strategy (Figure 8-4).

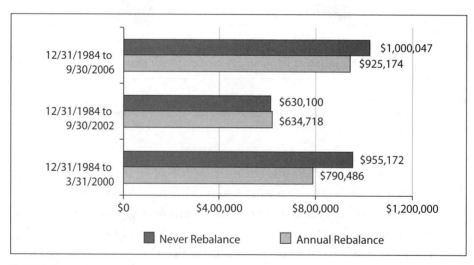

FIGURE 8–4 Mixed Results

Rebalancing can be made to look good or bad depending on what time period you're measuring.

Based on 60% stock / 30% bond / 10% cash portfolio starting with $100,000 in 1984. *Source:* T. Rowe Price

The point of all of this is, rebalancing can be made to look relatively rewarding or not, simply by adjusting the time period you're looking at. Regardless, another lesson of this example is that at the end of the day, there's surprisingly very little difference over the long run as to whether rebalancing makes you more money or not. Indeed, the T. Rowe Price research showed that the performance difference between a rebalanced and a non-rebalanced portfolio was even slimmer than Vanguard concluded. T. Rowe Price's research showed that the difference in approaches was just one-third of one percentage point annually.

What is clear, though—and what virtually every analysis of rebalancing shows—is that rebalancing periodically reduces the volatility of your investments and, ultimately, the risk of losing extreme amounts of money at inopportune times.

2. To Ensure that You Routinely Take Some Profits

When you rebalance—by selling some of your winning assets and buying some underperforming ones—you ensure that you periodically take some money off the table and book your gains. Why is this important?

Bull markets provide every investor with the potential for achieving sizable returns. But those who choose not to rebalance periodically risk missing out on converting those *paper* gains into actual profits (Table 8-4). Consider how easy it is to miss important opportunities. During the bull market of 2002–2007, for instance, the Standard & Poor's 500 index doubled from a low of 776 on October 9, 2002, to as high as 1,565 exactly five years later. Then, in the financial

TABLE 8–4 Highs and Lows *Bear markets have historically wiped out tremendous amounts of gains.*		
Bear Market	**S&P 500 High**	**S&P 500 Low**
10/2007 to 3/2009	1565.15	676.53
3/2000 to 10/2002	1527.46	776.76
7/1990 to 10/1990	368.95	295.46
8/1987 to 12/1987	336.77	223.92
11/1980 to 8/1982	140.52	102.42
1/1973 to 10/1974	120.24	62.28

Source: S&P

crisis, the S&P 500 sank, by March 2009, to as low as 676. In other words, if you never rebalanced between 2002 and 2009, you lost out on six and a half years' worth of stock market gains.

To be sure, the subsequent bull market would eventually return the S&P 500 to the 1,565 level and above. But the market did not return to those highs for another four years—until March 2013. By resetting your portfolio in a regular fashion, you make sure that opportunities such as this are always taken advantage of. Moreover, you make sure that you take advantage of them in quick order.

3. To Make Sure that You Always Sell High and Buy Low

The point of any investment strategy is to buy something for a low price and eventually sell it at a higher one. That's easier said than done. Rebalancing helps you toward this goal because the very essence of rebalancing is to trim your position in an asset class that's risen in value to such a degree that it now takes on disproportionate heft in your portfolio.

Remember too that there's another step involved. After reducing your exposure to an asset that has appreciated, rebalancing requires that you use those proceeds to buy an underperforming investment—in other words, an asset that is growing at a slower-than-average rate or that has fallen in value. In either case, this forces you to buy something at a low price.

This is an important point. History shows that the price you pay for an investment matters. The cheaper an investment is, based on its historic levels or fundamental factors such as corporate profits, the greater the likelihood that it will eventually rise in value once those attributes are fully appreciated by investors and reflected in the share price.

Not only does buying an undervalued investment help keep your losses low—since theoretically a cheap stock has less room to fall than an overpriced one—but the valuation of the security itself will help determine your expected returns. Indeed, researchers at the Vanguard Group found that one of the few fundamental factors that has real predictive power in gauging stock performance over the next 10 years is valuation.

Other market observers have come to a more direct conclusion: When it comes to stocks, the price you pay for your shares is a major determinant in your expected future gains. The lower the P/E of the stock you buy, the greater the likelihood that it will not only match the average historic performance of equities, but exceed it (Table 8-5).

TABLE 8–5 Valuations
Historically, stock market P/E ratios have been good at forecasting future long-term returns.

P/E Ratio (Based on 10-year average earnings)	Avg. Inflation-Adjusted Annual Return for Next 10 Years
5.2–9.6	10.3%
9.6–10.8	10.4%
10.8–11.9	10.4%
11.9–13.8	9.1%
13.8–15.7	8.0%
15.7–17.3	5.6%
17.3–18.9	5.3%
18.9–21.1	3.9%
21.1–25.1	0.9%
25.1 and higher	0.5%

Source: AQR Capital

Rebalancing Methods

There's a little secret when it comes to rebalancing that you need to know—and that's the fact that the actual method by which you reset your portfolio back to its intended mix actually doesn't make that big a difference.

Indeed, researchers at Washington Trust Bank studied the results of periodically resetting a 60 percent stock / 40 percent bond portfolio based on a variety of methods, including so-called time-based strategies as well as those that kick in when certain thresholds are met. They discovered that whether you rebalanced monthly, quarterly, or annually—or whether you reset your asset weightings if they drifted by a specific threshold (be that 1 percent, 2 percent, 10 percent, 20 percent, or 40 percent), the resulting performance was nearly identical. In almost all the cases they looked at over a span that stretched from 1978 to 2009, the results were annualized returns ranging from 10.4 percent to 10.6 percent.

Moreover, the various methods used to reset allocation strategies proved to be nearly identical when it comes to risk. The resulting portfolios' so-called standard deviation—which, again, measures volatility—was also nearly identical, ranging from a level of 10.4 to 10.9. As you can see, then, it really doesn't matter much.

The one variable that did change was cost. There are a couple of big downsides to rebalancing too frequently. The first, obviously, is that you don't give your investments enough time to run. So in the worst-case scenario, rebalancing too rapidly means you will miss out on potential gains. The other risk is that with a greater frequency of rebalancing, investors are forced to buy and sell more rapidly, and that drives up commission and trading costs, which eat into your performance.

The trick, then, is to strike a balance with your rebalancing strategy that suits your sensibilities.

Time-Based Rebalancing: Annual

Risk and Return Profile

Annual return: 10.49%

Returns less trading costs: 10.40%

Standard deviation: 10.6%

Turnover rate: 4%

Trading costs: 0.09% of assets

Of all the methods of adjusting your allocation strategy, annual rebalancing is the most common. For one thing, it's probably the easiest to remember. Many investors, for example, simply choose to automatically reset their allocations at the end of the year, on the first trading day of the year, or on their birthdays. Many brokerage accounts and 401(k) plans also have automated rebalancing tools on their websites that allow you to rebalance on a specific calendar date. The idea is simple. Say you start the year with a $100,000 portfolio, invested in a 60 percent stock / 40 percent bond mix. In other words, $60,000 of your money is in equities and $40,000 is in bonds. Now, assume that your stocks wind up advancing 25 percent this year, while your bonds stay flat, earning you zero percent. That means your $60,000 equity portfolio would now be worth $75,000, while your bonds would have remained at $40,000. Combined, your entire portfolio would now be worth $115,000. And since $75,000 of that is stocks, your asset allocation would have drifted to 65 percent stocks / 35 percent bonds.

How It Works

Under this scenario with annual rebalancing, you could simply wait until the end of the year, and on December 31 you would sell roughly $5,000 from your equity stake and use that money to boost your bonds so that you maintain a 40 percent weighting in fixed income.

It's up to you which equities you trim. You have several options as to how to do this.

Option 1

Trim equally from all your stocks and stock funds. Depending on how many separate securities you own, though, this may not be an ideal approach for you. That's because it could wind up being very costly, as it might mean processing a large number of separate trades to make a single rebalancing move. And that leads to large trading costs, which eat into your returns.

For example, say you own a dozen different stock funds, a dozen separate individual stocks, and a dozen bond funds. If you follow this approach to the letter, you could easily end up generating annual commission costs of more than $300, and some of those trades would be minuscule in size. This approach makes much more sense if you own, say, only two stock funds (for instance, one that covers the broad U.S. market and a separate international stock fund). In that case, your annual commissions would be closer to $20 a year.

It also makes sense if all or most of your portfolio is held in tax-advantaged 401(k) retirement plans and individual retirement plans (IRAs). That's because basic trades in those accounts are commission-free events. In fact, if you have most of your money in tax-sheltered retirement plans, it's best to do the bulk of your rebalancing there.

Option 2

Sell $5,000 from just those equities and equity funds that have posted the biggest gains. The benefit here is that you would be taking profits from those investments that have advanced the most, thereby reducing the risk of owning overly expensive securities. The downside of this approach is that you would be realizing the most capital gains, which would trigger immediate capital gains taxes on those sales. The one exception is that if you were rebalancing through a 401(k) or IRA, such trades would be considered nontaxable events (in addition to being free of broker-age commissions).

Option 3

Sell $5,000 from those stocks and stock funds that have lost money. Now, this may seem counterintuitive, especially since the point of rebalancing is to sell assets that have outperformed to buy those that have underperformed. But selling money-losing investments within an asset class that has risen in overall value actually has some merits.

For starters, it allows you to maintain your overall allocation strategy—in this example, a 60 percent weighting to stocks. It allows those investments that are doing well to keep running, which means you can enjoy some of the momentum in the market. Finally, by selling a money-losing investment, you can realize a capital loss. And as bad as it sounds to turn a paper loss into a real one, the fact that Uncle Sam will help defray some of those losses is appealing.

The Internal Revenue Service allows investors to use losses to offset capital gains elsewhere in their portfolios, thereby reducing overall tax liabilities. If you don't have any capital gains to offset in a particular year, you can offset up to $3,000 of ordinary income with those losses. And if your losses exceed that amount, you can carry forward those tax-advantaged losses to use in future tax years to offset future gains.

The Pros of Annual Rebalancing

- **It's convenient.** Of all the methods, this one probably requires the least effort. You can simply do this on your birthday or at the end or start of the year.

- **It requires the fewest trades.** When Washington Mutual Trust examined the implementation of various rebalancing techniques from 1978 to 2009, researchers found that of all the major methods, this one required the fewest trades by far.

- **It's cheap.** Because of the fewer trades, this rebalancing method ends up costing the least of all the major methods, resulting in expenses of about 0.09 percent of assets.

- **It gives your investments time to perform.** Of all the basic timing methods, this gives your investments at least a full year to run. This is important because of the potential gains you can earn. It's also important because of the tax implications.

- If your gains are held for longer than a year, they will qualify as long-term gains, which are taxed at a maximum rate of 15 percent (or 0 percent if you're in the 10 or 15 percent income tax bracket).

- If your gains are held for less time, they are considered short-term gains and taxed at the ordinary income tax rate, which could run as high as 35 percent.

The Cons of Annual Rebalancing

- **It's imprecise.** There's nothing special about this method of rebalancing, as it simply selects a random date for making adjustments (Table 8-6). A person who selects January 1 for rebalancing may end up with slightly different results from someone who selects June 30.

- **You're not assured of hitting all the turns.** Say this is the year 2000 and you rebalance at the end of every year. The bear market of 2000–2002 began in March of that year, not in December. That year, the market ended up rebalancing for you, and in a way that you probably did not like.

Time-Based Rebalancing: Monthly

Risk and Return Profile

Annual returns: 10.38 percent

Returns less trading costs: 10.13 percent

Standard deviation: 10.6 percent

Turnover rate: 12 percent

Trading costs: 0.25 percent of assets

TABLE 8–6 Time-Based Rebalancing *The pros and cons of various time-based rebalancing strategies*				
	Monthly	**Quarterly**	**Semiannual**	**Annual**
Annual Returns	10.38%	10.46%	10.59%	10.49%
Annual Trading Costs	0.25%	0.15%	0.12%	0.09%
Returns Minus Trading Costs	10.13%	10.31%	10.47%	10.40%
Standard Deviation	10.62	10.58	10.54	10.63
Number of Trades	370	124	62	31
Annual Turnover	12.39%	7.72%	5.90%	4.06%

Source: Based on 60% stock / 40% bond strategy since 1978; Washington Trust Bank Wealth Management

The Pros of Monthly Rebalancing

- **It's still convenient.** While not as easy as annual rebalancing, monthly rebalancing allows you to simply glance at your month-end brokerage statements and use that data to figure out exactly how to reset your allocation.

- **It maintains the most discipline.** While annual rebalancing lets your portfolio drift for 12 months, monthly rebalancing maintains a much tighter range, so that your portfolio is constantly providing the risk/reward profile that you seek.

The Cons of Monthly Rebalancing

- **It's expensive.** When Washington Mutual Trust examined the implementation of various rebalancing techniques from 1978 to 2009, monthly rebalancing triggered the highest number of trades—in fact, 10 times the number of trades required to implement an annual rebalancing strategy. This, of course, led to the highest costs of any of the most common rebalancing methods, reducing your returns by a quarter of a percentage point each year.

- **It's time consuming.** To undertake this frequency of rebalancing, you have to monitor your portfolio every month, which not all investors have the time to do.

- **It delivers slightly lower returns.** There are a couple of reasons why monthly rebalancing produced slightly lower returns than other basic strategies. For starters, it's more expensive, and trading costs reduce your portfolio's net gains dollar for dollar. Moreover, because a monthly strategy gives rising investments only 30 days to climb before being pared back, it is unlikely to outperform annual rebalancing or no rebalancing in a rising market.

- **There's no discernible improvement in volatility.** Even though monthly rebalancing maintains more discipline over your portfolio, there was no discernible reduction in volatility. In fact, researchers at Vanguard studied monthly and annual rebalancing going back to 1926 and found that a portfolio that's reset once a month actually has an ever-so-slightly higher standard deviation than an annually rebalanced strategy. Washington Trust studied rebalancing in more recent years and came to the same conclusion. The standard deviation of a monthly rebalanced 60 percent stock / 40 percent bond portfolio was 10.6 between 1978 and 2009. That was one-tenth of a percent higher than the standard deviation for an annually rebalanced 60/40 portfolio.

Performance-Based Rebalancing: 10 Percent Threshold

Risk and Return Profile

Annual returns: 10.54 percent

Returns less trading costs: 10.43 percent

Standard deviation: 10.6 percent

Turnover rate: 6 percent

Trading costs: 0.11 percent of assets

Unlike annual or monthly rebalancing, which use time as a trigger to adjust, dynamic rebalancing techniques focus on the actual drift in your portfolio. For example, let's assume that your portfolio shifts slightly over the course of a year from, say, a 70 percent stock / 30 percent bond allocation to a 72 percent stock / 28 percent bond mix. And let's assume that you adhere to an annual rebalancing regimen.

Because such a strategy is rather indiscriminate, you would be forced to make an adjustment to your portfolio at the end of the year even though your portfolio shifted by only 2 percentage points (or 3 percent based on the 70 percent allocation to stocks). Assuming that you had a $100,000 portfolio, $72,000 of which was held in equities, you would be talking about an adjustment to your portfolio based on a drift of just $2,000 in your stock weighting.

Threshold-based rebalancing addresses this problem by only requiring that an adjustment be made if there's a substantial shift in your portfolio (Table 8-7). A common threshold-based strategy requires a tweak only if your stock allocation

TABLE 8–7 Threshold-Based Rebalancing
The pros and cons of various threshold-based rebalancing strategies.

	1%	2%	10%	20%	30%	40%
Annual Returns	10.39%	10.39%	10.54%	10.51%	10.51%	10.44%
Annual Trading Costs	0.25%	0.21%	0.11%	0.04%	0.05%	0.03%
Returns Minus Trading Costs	10.14%	10.18%	10.43%	10.47%	10.46%	10.41%
Standard Deviation	10.62	10.62	10.62	10.65	10.74	10.89
Number of Trades	367	345	144	39	28	13
Annual Turnover	12.08%	10.74%	5.82%	2.55%	2.22%	1.22%

Source: Based on 60% stock / 40% bond strategy since 1978; Washington Trust Bank Wealth Management

moves by 10 percent (not percentage points). In other words, if you keep 70 percent of your money allocated to stocks and your equity weighting falls to less than 63 percent of your portfolio or climbs to above 77 percent, only then would you make a shift.

Similarly, if you have 50 percent allocated to equities, you would make a move only if that allocation drives below 45 percent (since that's a 10 percent change from your original 50 percent weighting) or climbs above 55 percent.

The Pros of 10 Percent Threshold Rebalancing

- **It requires rebalancing only when needed.** Unlike time-based methods, this strategy requires action only when substantial changes are necessary. This means that you will never have to make unnecessary adjustments to your portfolio. In fact, in years in which stocks and bonds are relatively flat, post below-average gains, or deliver similar returns—think years like 2004, 2005, and 2011—there may not be a need to rebalance for more than a couple of years, which would be cost-effective.

- **It lets your investments run.** By letting your asset allocations drift by a full 10 percent, you can enjoy the full benefits of what stocks are delivering in a typical year's performance—without having to rebalance if stocks post below-average returns. The bottom line: 10 percent rebalancing has posted the highest annual returns of any of the major rebalancing strategies based on data going back to 1978.

- **It's cheap.** The annual cost of this method of rebalancing, based on actual market conditions dating back to 1978, has been around 0.11 percent of assets each year on average, which is nearly as cheap as annual rebalancing. Plus, it's less than half as expensive as monthly rebalancing.

The Cons of 10 Percent Threshold Rebalancing

- **It requires attention.** While time-based methods are easy to remember, since you can literally mark your rebalancing date on a calendar, threshold-based strategies require you to constantly pay attention to your portfolio and to do the necessary math. So if you're not comfortable putting your portfolio into a spreadsheet or website and paying routine attention to your mix, then you should probably stick to annual rebalancing.

- **You may have to rebalance more than once a year.** In years in which stocks or bonds rise more than usual—think 1996, 1997, 1998, 1999, 2003, and 2009— you may actually have to readjust your mix twice or perhaps even more.

Performance-Based Rebalancing: 25 Percent Threshold

Risk and Return Profile

Annual returns: 10.51 percent

Returns less trading costs: 10.47 percent

Standard deviation: 10.7 percent

Turnover rate: 3 percent

Trading costs: 0.04 percent of assets

The Pros of 25 Percent Threshold Rebalancing

- **It really lets your investments run.** Just as with 10 percent threshold rebalancing, this method requires you to make adjustments to your portfolio only when there are significant swings in your allocation—in this case, really significant. This threshold-based strategy forces a move only when your equity allocation shifts by 25 percent (again, this is percent, not percentage points).

- In other words, if you have a 50 percent stock / 50 percent bond weighting, you would rebalance only when your equities fall to 37.5 percent of your total portfolio or rise above an allocation of 62.5 percent. With a 60 percent equity weighting, rebalancing kicks in only when your stock exposure drops below 45 percent or rises above 75 percent. And with a 70 percent stock weighting, you would make a move only when your stocks fall to below 62.5 percent or climb above 87.5 percent.

- **It's really cheap.** Because this strategy allows for such wild swings in your strategy, it is extremely low cost. The average annual expense for 25 percent rebalancing is a minuscule 0.04 percent.

The Cons of 25 Percent Threshold Rebalancing

- **It may expose your portfolio to more risk than you're comfortable with.** Under this approach, a person who begins with a moderate 60 percent stock weighting could easily wind up with a very conservative 45 percent weighting in equities or a very aggressive 75 percent plan before ever making a single adjustment. If you're in your late 50s, for example, and are fearful of suffering big losses in your portfolio at the very end of your investing career, this strategy may not be the right one for you.

- **You may miss opportunities to take profits.** With a range this wide, there will be times when a 25 percent rebalancing strategy actually misses an entire profit cycle. For example, say you start with a 60 percent equity weighting, and because of a bull market, that allocation rises to 72 percent. This would represent a 20 percent swing, just shy of triggering the automatic rebalancing. Now assume that the bull market ends and a new bear market begins, cutting your 72 percent equity weighting down to 50 percent. Both swings fell short of a 25 percent shift, so on both the upside and the downside, you would have been left sitting idle, in effect letting the market rebalance for you.

A Hybrid Approach

As a result of the shortcomings of all of these approaches, many financial planners now recommend a compromise solution that is part time-based and part threshold-based. In this case, you would still rebalance on a specific date in the calendar year, as with annual rebalancing. But with this hybrid method, you would make adjustments to your plan only if your equity weighting shifted by a certain amount in that time period—say, 10 percent. In this case, you would still look to rebalance on the same day annually, making for an extremely simple approach. Because you would make a move only if a significant shift took place, though, you would allow your investments to run for potentially more than a year—lowering your costs and hopefully turning a slightly bigger profit.

QUIZ

1. **Rebalancing is a technique to ...**
   A. Maximize your gains.
   B. Maximize your risks.
   C. Maintain your gains.
   D. Maintain your risk.

2. **If you failed to rebalance in the late 1990s, your 60 percent stock / 40 percent bond allocation would have turned into ...**
   A. 40 percent stocks / 60 percent bonds.
   B. 50 percent stocks / 50 percent bonds.
   C. 80 percent stocks / 20 percent bonds.

3. **If you fail to rebalance and your portfolio loses 50 percent of its value, how much would your portfolio have to gain to break even?**
   A. 25 percent
   B. 50 percent
   C. 75 percent
   D. 100 percent

4. **Routinely rebalancing your stock exposure is important because bear markets typically materialize every ...**
   A. 3 years.
   B. 5 years.
   C. 10 years.
   D. 25 years.

5. **You make more money rebalancing than by not rebalancing?**
   A. Always
   B. Never
   C. Sometimes

6. **Which method of rebalancing makes you the most money?**
   A. Time-based
   B. Threshold-based
   C. Neither

7. **What is a major shortcoming of monthly rebalancing?**
   A. It's too costly
   B. It's too risky
   C. It's not risky enough

8. **What is a major shortcoming of threshold-based rebalancing?**
   A. You may not adjust your portfolio for more than a year
   B. You may have to adjust your portfolio multiple times a year
   C. Neither
   D. Both

9. **A 25 percent threshold-based rebalancing strategy could expose you to ...**
   A. Too much risk.
   B. Too many gains.
   C. Too few gains.

10. **Rebalancing forces you to ...**
    A. Buy low and sell low.
    B. Buy low and sell high.
    C. Buy high and sell high.
    D. Buy high and sell low

chapter 9

Automating Your Asset Allocation Strategy

Establishing an asset allocation strategy does not have to be a "do-it-yourself" exercise. These days, the investment management world is awash in mutual funds and exchange-traded funds available to the retail public that will make some or all of these decisions for you. These funds aren't necessarily appropriate for all investors, especially if you believe you have the wherewithal to pick stocks better than the pros (or to pick individual stock and bond funds better than professionals). Still, they're worth considering as a simple solution to satisfy some, most, or all of your asset allocation needs.

Some professionally managed funds will alleviate the burden of having to decide whether to overweight stocks or bonds at the moment based on the current short-term market environment. Others will help you establish a level of equities that's appropriate for your circumstances. Still others will implement a strategy for you once you decide how conservative or aggressive you want to be.

It is important to understand how each of the three major types of asset allocation funds work, because depending on which option you choose, you may still have some work to do to customize these off-the-shelf strategies. Also, before you choose to invest in a ready-made asset allocation fund, you must decide whether you will be turning over all the decision making in your portfolio to these funds, or whether you want to preserve some decision-making role for yourself.

This is an important consideration. Here's why: Let's say that you opt to go with an asset allocation fund with a 60 percent stock / 40 percent bond strategy, but only put half of your investable assets into it. With the rest of your money, assume that you choose to invest in a mix of individual stocks and stock funds of your own choosing, believing that you can add some additional value with your own skills and knowledge.

In that case, what you've done is taken an original 60 percent stock / 40 percent bond mix and turned it into an 80 percent stock / 20 percent bond mix because you chose to invest half of your money in an all-stock strategy. Now, that may have been your intent all along. And in that case, there's nothing wrong with morphing the strategy set out by that asset allocation fund. This sort of mixing and matching approach—where you use an asset allocation fund to satisfy some of your needs, but you build a customized cluster of individual securities or funds around it—is a totally legitimate way to use these investment vehicles.

However, if this was not your stated intent, you must know how your own decision making can alter the path that you may have sought by picking an asset allocation fund to begin with.

With that in mind, let's consider the different types of asset allocation funds at your disposal—discussing both their benefits and their shortcomings.

Option 1: Old-Fashioned Balanced Funds

These off-the-shelf funds automatically give you exposure to stocks and bonds through a single portfolio.

What Are They?

As their name implies, these funds invest in a "balance" of stocks and bonds. Traditionally, that balance starts off somewhere close to a 60 percent stock / 40 percent bond mix. In the case of T. Rowe Price Balanced, the stated mix is 65 percent equities and 35 percent fixed income.

The Vanguard Balanced Fund, on the other hand, adheres exactly to the classic 60 percent stock / 40 percent bond mix by prospectus (Table 9-1).

TABLE 9–1 A Balanced Approach—10-Year Annual Returns
A balanced 60% stock / 40% bond strategy has delivered most of the returns of stocks with a fraction of the risk.

Strategy	10-Year Annual Returns	10-Year Standard Deviation
Vanguard Balanced Fund	7.1%	9.3
Vanguard 500 Stock	7.7%	14.7
Vanguard Total Bond Market	4.5%	3.4

Source: Morningstar

This means that over the course of any given year, this fund's managers will be directed by the bylaws of the Fund to adjust the portfolio back to that goal as the differing performance of stocks and bonds tweaks that mix from time to time. This may sound like a humdrum approach to investing, but there are clear advantages.

Advantage 1: You Know What You're Getting

If you think that a 60 percent stock / 40 percent bond mix is well suited to you, and you want the reassurance that at least once a year—and sometimes even more frequently—your fund will rebalance your portfolio back to that intended target, then a traditional balanced fund can work to your benefit. This will help you use such a balanced fund more effectively. If, for instance, this fund simply represents the core part of your portfolio, and you intend to build other funds around it to get a more diversified mix, then knowing what your balanced fund's asset allocation is at all times will be a big advantage.

Advantage 2: There Is Something to a 60/40 Mix

A traditional 60 percent stock / 40 percent bond balanced fund used to be a staple of investment management, but in recent decades—especially after the explosive growth of stocks in the 1980s and 1990s—investors grew to believe that such a strategy was old-fashioned. At a time when equities were in some years posting 20 percent plus annual returns, why take nearly half of your money and stuff it in much slower growing bonds?

Of course, that attitude took a bit of a hit in the 2000s, when equities went nowhere for more than a decade while bonds continued a nice run. Now there is growing research that says that a 60 percent stock / 40 percent bond strategy may, over the long run, take care of most of your investment needs.

Indeed, analysts at Morningstar recently observed the performance of the Vanguard Balanced Fund and concluded, "The portfolio has provided above-average returns with below-average risk. Over the past 10 years, Vanguard Balanced has provided 95 percent of the return of the S&P 500 but only 63 percent of the risk." Morningstar went on to note that while many investors may have felt disillusioned in the financial crisis, when this diversified approach still lost 22 percent, that was still far less than the 37 percent loss suffered by the S&P 500. Moreover, "patient investors recouped their losses in less than two years."

An analysis by Vanguard also concluded that during the financial crisis years of 2007 to early 2009, an investment in a simple 60 percent stock / 40 percent bond portfolio would have done you better—in some cases far better—than using exotic and expensive hedge fund strategies (Table 9-2). What's more, this simple strategy outperformed those same hedge fund strategies once the market started getting going in 2009, 2010, and 2011.

Advantage 3: They're Not Just Diversified, They're Fully Diversified

The true benefit of balanced funds is that they give you instant diversification between stocks and bonds (Figure 9-1). Another advantage is how well diversified they are within their stock and bond holdings.

TABLE 9–2 A Balanced Approach—Crash and Rally Performance
A balanced 60% stock / 40% bond strategy held its own in the financial panic, and thrived in the subsequent rally.

Strategy	Crash Performance 11/07 to 2/09	Rally Performance 3/09 to 12/11
60% Stock / 40% Bonds	−25.4%	17.9%
Emerging Markets Hedge	−25.4%	12.1%
Market Neutral Hedge	−33.9%	4.4%
Event-Driven Hedge	−14.7%	7.8%
Long-Short Hedge	−17.0%	7.5%

Source: Vanguard

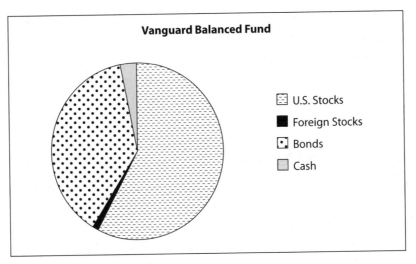

FIGURE 9–1 A Balanced Approach
The Vanguard Balanced Fund offers instant exposure to all core asset classes.

Source: Morningstar

For instance, here's what you get when you make one decision to buy the Vanguard Balanced Fund: About 72 percent of your equities are held in large-cap stocks, while 28 percent are held in mid-sized, small-, and extremely small micro-cap stocks. Also, 90 percent of your equities are in U.S. shares, but 10 percent are held in companies based overseas. What's more, this fund, like most balanced funds, will give you broad-based exposure to all 10 major sectors of the economy: technology, financials, industrials, materials, consumer discretionary, consumer staples, healthcare, energy, telecommunications, and utilities. Within the bond portion of the portfolio, the fund invests nearly half its fixed-income assets in government securities, around a quarter in corporate debt, and the remaining quarter in mortgage-backed bonds.

Other funds are even more diversified. The T. Rowe Price Balanced Fund, for example, keeps as much as one-third of its equity stake in foreign stocks, while using the remaining two-thirds to hold domestic shares. T. Rowe Price also offers even deeper exposure to other types of fixed-income securities, adding small doses of high-yielding junk bonds, municipal debt, and even foreign fixed-income to the mix.

Advantage 4: They're Simple

Perhaps the biggest advantage of a balanced fund over other types of asset allocation portfolios is that these vehicles require the least amount of decision making on your part. You do not have to come to a balanced fund knowing your preference for risk, your tolerance for risk taking, or what your time horizon should be. Because it is a one-size-fits-all type of fund, you take it for what it is—a simple one-decision fund that gains you quick, simple, and nearly complete exposure to the major asset classes that you'll need to populate at least the core part of your portfolio.

What Are Their Shortcomings?

What makes a balanced fund so simple and popular is also one of the biggest criticisms. These are not customized products that suit your individual needs. Rather, they are mass-marketed investment vehicles that are designed to appeal to the broadest audience possible. That means that if you're in your 30s and want to take more risks with equities, a balanced fund will not be the best vehicle to do that because it must also appeal to investors in their 50s and 60s, who demand and require greater fixed-income exposure. Similarly, if you are a retiree in your 70s who is seeking to preserve principal while simultaneously drawing down income, a balanced fund won't be your best bet because such funds have to keep a decent amount of their assets in stocks to assure a basic level of growth that appeals to younger audiences.

What other problems will you encounter when using a balanced fund?

Problem 1: They're Not All 60/40

There is no rule under the Investment Company Act of 1940 that states that a balanced fund must adhere to a 60 percent stock / 40 percent bond strategy. As stated earlier, the T. Rowe Price Balanced Fund, for one, goes with a 65 percent stocks and 35 percent bond mix.

The variations only grow from there. On the one hand, there's the Ivy Balanced Fund, for instance, which as of late 2013 kept more than 70 percent of its assets in equities and less than 30 percent in bonds and cash. At the other end, you have a fund like Weitz Balanced, which invested only around 40 percent of its assets in equities (as of November 2013), with another 40 percent in cash and just 20 percent in fixed income.

The challenge is that without a clear, industrywide definition of what a balanced fund is, it is up to the investors to investigate which funds—and which underlying investment strategies—are best suited for them. You can look up a fund's approach through its prospectus, which is often found on the fund company website. Or you can go to a site such as Morningstar.com. This data-rich fund site keeps tabs on the current portfolios of all major mutual and exchange-traded funds. To see how a fund is currently weighted, just type in its name or ticker symbol, click on Morningstar's "Portfolio" tab, and then drill down to see the fund's holdings in stocks, bonds, and other asset classes.

Even if you find the information you seek, there is another issue that you must contend with. While some funds state in their prospectus that they will adhere to a stated strategy, most give their managers a wide berth to switch their strategy from time to time, as market conditions warrant.

That brings us to the next concern …

Problem 2: Even If a Balanced Fund Starts at 60/40, It's Not Obliged to Stay There

There is no rule under the Investment Company Act of 1940 that states that a balanced fund that starts out with a 60 percent stock / 40 percent bond mix must continue to adhere to that strategy on a permanent basis. While some funds may indicate a preferential strategy that they plan to adhere to over time, few commit to a single asset allocation strategy in their prospectus. Those that do are obliged to stay the course. The vast majority, though, do not explicitly promise a specific asset allocation strategy. They may set a range of stock allocations that they can follow, but that range is often fairly wide.

Keep in mind that funds, like all financial products, are created to be sold to the general public in mass quantities. That means that balanced funds must be designed in a way that appeals to would-be investors who are looking for the best-performing options at any given moment of time.

Not surprisingly, during the go-go period for stocks in the 1990s—before the tech stock crash—many balanced funds quietly shifted from the traditional 60 percent stock / 40 percent bond mix to a 70 percent stock / 30 percent bond mix. In some cases, that stock creep took portfolios to three-quarters equities and just one-quarter bonds. The result: By boosting their exposure to equities at a time when stocks were outperforming other asset classes, risk-taking balanced funds generated better-than-average returns, making themselves stand out in annual charts and lists of top-performing investment vehicles.

Also not surprisingly, when the stock market collapsed starting in 2000 and fixed income became the dominant investment between 2000 and 2011, many of those same balanced funds dialed back their exposure to equities from 70 percent or so down to 60 percent and in some cases even less. That allowed market-timing balanced fund managers to stand out at a time when fixed-income investments were the only assets making money.

This means that when it comes to a balanced fund, you have a couple of choices. You can be hypervigilant by researching which ones not only will provide exposure to the asset allocation you seek, but will also adhere to it over time. Or you have to be willing to accept wider swings in your portfolio that might take you from conservative territory (say, 55 percent or 60 percent stocks) all the way to aggressive territory (70 percent to 75 percent equities).

Problem 3: Different Balanced Funds Will Arrive at the Same Asset Allocation Goal Differently

Even if you are successful at locating balanced funds with the right mix for you, there's another challenge: Does the fund implement the strategy in a way that you agree with?

For instance, most funds are actively managed, which means that the balanced fund managers will determine which asset allocation strategy to go with. And to implement their plan, the managers will likely select a combination of individual stocks and bonds, and actively trade into and out of those stocks and bonds to try to generate the performance they seek. However, there are many variations of this approach.

In some cases, the active manager may decide that the best way to implement his or her strategy is not by buying individual stocks and bonds, but by owning a combination of individual securities and mutual funds. In still other cases, the active manager may choose to enact the strategy with a series of index funds that are not actively managed at all, but rather are passive investment vehicles. An example of this is the Schwab MarketTrack Balanced Portfolio, whose underlying holdings are four index portfolios: the Schwab S&P 500 Index Fund, the Schwab Small Cap Index Fund, the Schwab International Index Fund, and the Schwab Total Bond Market Fund. And in still other cases, there isn't an active approach to the balanced fund at all, but rather a mechanistic approach that adheres to a preset mix of stocks and bonds and implements and rebalances back to that strategy in a routine manner using all index funds.

Your challenge as an investor is to determine which of these methods of investment management you're dealing with in the funds you come across and which method you're comfortable with when it comes to your own portfolio.

How They Can Be Used?

The best use of a balanced fund is in a hub-and-spoke manner, where it serves as the core part of your portfolio, delivering the basic range of exposure to stocks and bonds that you seek. Then around that core, you can populate your portfolio with other investments that are meant to explore other assets that can supplement that balanced fund.

For example, as diversified as most balanced funds are, many don't have much exposure to foreign emerging market stocks. In the case of Vanguard Balanced, a mere 0.02 percent of the stock portion of the fund is held in shares of stocks based in the fast-growing economies of Asia, Latin America, and Eastern Europe. The rest is invested in the much slower-growing developed economies of the United States, Western Europe, and Japan. The Fidelity Balanced Fund has barely more exposure to developing economies, but it also has extremely light weightings in small-cap U.S. stocks as well as junk bonds. For its part, T. Rowe Price Balanced has more than 2 percent exposure to the emerging markets, but it too lacks much exposure to small-cap equities. And all three funds generally lack exposure to foreign small-cap shares, international bonds, and municipal debt.

As with any good "core and explore" strategy, then, you can use the balanced fund as the foundation of your portfolio. Normally, building your asset allocation foundation takes many decisions, including not just what the mix of your stocks and bonds will be, but also the infinite decisions in determining how to implement that strategy. It's like building the foundation of a house. Not only must you establish architectural plans for the dimensions of the foundation and how thick the foundation walls will be, but you normally have to establish an actual construction plan for which crews will come in first to get construction underway.

Using this metaphor, think of a balanced fund foundation as modular housing. The fund itself is a prebuilt foundation that's constructed off-site and trucked to your construction site. Once it is in place in your portfolio, you can get work crews to start building the rest of the house—or you can do it yourself.

What is far rarer is to use the balanced fund as the entirety of your strategy. This is partly because most balanced funds, as was just mentioned, aren't hemmed in by their bylaws. Or at the very least, they are not hemmed in enough to be trusted to stick with a specific asset allocation strategy throughout time to make planning simple.

Option 2: Risk-Based Asset Allocation Funds

These are all-in-one funds that use your tolerance for risk taking to tailor a strategy that's best suited for you.

What Are They?

You may have come across these mutual funds with somewhat odd names. These are funds like American Century Strategic Allocation: Moderate, Transamerica Asset Allocation Growth, or Columbia Capital Allocation Conservative. These all-in-one portfolios are like balanced funds, though most of them also add exposure to that third asset class: cash.

Another difference is that—unlike balanced funds, which may start with a 60 percent stock / 40 percent bond strategy but have the ability to change—risk-based asset allocation funds announce to the public what their strategy will be going forward. At the very least, they generally inform you whether the fund will take an aggressive, moderate, or conservative approach to its equity exposure.

This is why these funds are usually separated out into three different categories by fund trackers such as Morningstar: Aggressive Allocation, Moderate Allocation, and Conservative Allocation.

Conservative Allocation

You can pretty much guess to whom these asset allocation funds are geared: mostly older investors who cannot keep the bulk of their assets in stocks, but also risk-averse investors who simply choose not to keep too much of their portfolio in equities. In fact, Morningstar's definition of a conservative allocation fund is as follows:

> Conservative-allocation portfolios seek to provide both capital appreciation and income by investing in three major areas: stocks, bonds, and cash. These portfolios tend to hold smaller positions in stocks than moderate-allocation portfolios. These portfolios typically have 20% to 50% of assets in equities and 50% to 80% of assets in fixed income and cash.

The key is that these funds will generally keep less than half of their assets in equities. This means that they are really geared only for older investors who are either nearing retirement or already retired—or for folks who do not require the type of long-term growth that only stocks can provide.

Traditionally, these funds target around 40 percent stock exposure, but as with balanced funds, different portfolios can vary wildly in their strategy and decision making. For example, on the one hand, you have a fund like Columbia Capital Allocation Conservative, with just 20 percent equity exposure and 80 percent exposure to bonds and cash. On the other hand, American Century Strategic Allocation: Conservative keeps more than 45 percent of its assets in equities, and within equities, it keeps a fair amount in riskier small stocks and foreign shares.

Moderate Allocation

Moderate risk asset allocation funds target the majority of investors, who believe that they need a majority of their portfolio to be held in growth-oriented equities, but aren't so aggressive as to keep three-quarters or more of their portfolios in equities. This is generally for folks who are in their 30s, 40s, and even 50s. Morningstar's definition of a moderate allocation fund is as follows:

> *Moderate-allocation portfolios seek to provide both capital appreciation and income by investing in three major areas: stocks, bonds, and cash. These portfolios tend to hold larger positions in stocks than conservative-allocation portfolios. These portfolios typically have 50% to 70% of assets in equities and the remainder in fixed income and cash.*

Because of their moderate stake in equities, these funds are generally suited for the bulk of the investing population. However, it is important to note that the definition of moderate runs a fairly broad range. And sometimes, that range can pierce the general guidelines that Morningstar has established.

For example, in November 2013, SCS Tactical Allocation Fund, which Morningstar classifies as a moderate allocation portfolio, held 82 percent of its assets in equities (and 75 percentage points of that allocation was in U.S. stocks), with less than 5 percent in bonds and the remainder in cash. This doesn't mean that that fund will forever be that exposed to stocks, but at that moment in time, the managers of SCS Tactical determined that that was the best course of action.

At the very same time, though, other moderate allocation managers viewed the markets in an entirely different light. The managers of Nuveen Intelligent Risk Moderate Allocation, for example, held only 50 percent in equities (with only around 30 percentage points in domestic shares), with the other half in bonds and other assets.

It is thus incumbent on the investor to investigate how "moderate" a moderate allocation fund will be.

Aggressive Allocation

Aggressive risk asset allocation funds target a significantly younger audience who have the sufficient time horizon and risk tolerance to seek growth but also to stomach the short-term losses that a vastly majority equity strategy can lead to. According to Morningstar, here is the definition of what an aggressive allocation fund is:

> *Aggressive-allocation portfolios seek to provide both capital appreciation and income by investing in three major areas: stocks, bonds, and cash. These portfolios tend to hold larger positions in stocks than moderate-allocation portfolios. These portfolios typically have 70% to 90% of assets in equities and the remainder in fixed income and cash.*

Here again, you have to be willing to accept as much as 90 percent or more of your portfolio in equities. Moreover, even though aggressive allocation funds are supposed to be exposed to all the major asset classes, not all of these funds will offer a substantial allocation to fixed income. The Nuveen Intelligent Risk Growth Allocation fund, for example, held 90 percent of its assets in equities as of late 2013. But the fund actually held virtually nothing in cash or bonds, preferring instead at the time to wager on commodities (such as gold and other natural resources) and real estate via real estate investment trusts and other real estate companies.

Over the past five years, a period that witnessed a historically strong bull market for stocks, aggressive risk asset allocation funds posted stellar results of nearly 16 percent a year, on average, owing largely to their oversized exposure to equities. By comparison, moderate allocation funds, with slightly less exposure to stocks, did slightly worse (13% annually). And conservative allocation funds, with even less weighting to equities and large stakes in bonds and cash, did even worse (11% annually) (Table 9-3).

World Allocation

There is one more type of risk-based asset allocation fund to consider. World allocation funds also attempt to strike a balance between stocks, bonds, and cash,

TABLE 9–3 Asset Allocation Variations
How different levels of aggressiveness performed over various time periods.

	2008	Past 3 Years	Past 5 Years
Aggressive Allocation	–34.3%	10.4%	17.5%
Moderate Allocation	–28.0%	9.6%	15.5%
Conservative Allocation	–18.6%	6.3%	11.9%

Source: Morningstar

but as their name would indicate, world allocation funds tend to be more globally diversified than other balanced portfolios. This is Morningstar's definition of a world allocation fund:

> *World-allocation portfolios seek to provide both capital appreciation and income by investing in three major areas: stocks, bonds, and cash. While these portfolios do explore the whole world, most of them focus on the U.S., Canada, Japan, and the larger markets in Europe. It is rare for such portfolios to invest more than 10% of their assets in emerging markets. These portfolios typically have at least 10% of assets in bonds, less than 70% of assets in stocks, and at least 40% of assets in non-U.S. stocks or bonds.*

A classic example is T. Rowe Price Global Allocation, which keeps around 60 percent of its assets in equities, 30 percent in a mix of bonds and cash, and the rest in alternative assets. Within that 60 percent equity exposure, though, more than half comes from foreign stocks. And within that mix, more than 10 percent is held in emerging market shares. Similarly, within T. Rowe Price Global Allocation's fixed-income weighting, only about 60 percent is invested in U.S. government and corporate bonds, with the remaining 40 percent being invested in government and corporate debt of Western Europe, Eastern Europe, Asia, Latin America, Canada, and Mexico.

The difficulty with choosing a world allocation fund is that while you know you're going to be getting widespread global diversity, you have to research how conservative or aggressive each individual fund in this grouping is likely to be. The swings can be far wider than for conservative, moderate, or aggressive allocation funds.

For example, on the one hand, you have a fund like Quaker Global Tactical Allocation, which in late 2013 held nearly 100 percent of its assets in stocks. And within its equity stake, more than a third was invested overseas, with two-thirds in domestic shares. By comparison, the MFS Global Multi-Asset Fund recently held only around 35 percent of its stake in stocks, which were evenly split between domestic and international shares. The remaining two-thirds of the MFS fund was held in bonds and cash.

The Pros of Asset Allocation Funds

Asset allocation funds are one-decision portfolios that allow you to gain instant diversification. Moreover, many asset allocation funds are more diversified than balanced funds are, and provide exposure not just to stocks and bonds, but also to cash and in many instance alternative assets such as real estate and commodities.

A further benefit: Despite their differing approaches to stocks and bonds, asset allocation funds still adhere to a tighter range of equity exposure than balanced funds. That means that as long as you know what strategy you want to undertake, you can better customize your approach through an asset allocation fund than via a balanced portfolio.

And for as long as you decide to hold onto that conservative, moderate, or aggressive asset allocation fund, the portfolio will rebalance your holdings for you within that same category of risk. This means that the only work you need to do with a risk-based asset allocation fund is decide what your risk tolerance is. Then, over the next several years, you'll need to revisit that decision only if you determine that your risk tolerance or appetite has changed over time—for instance, because you've grown older or your life circumstances have changed.

The Problem with Asset Allocation Funds

As simple and as easy as asset allocation funds are, they do have some shortcomings. The first is that they force investors to determine what level of risk they ought to be taking, and surveys consistently show that investors incorrectly gauge their own true risk tolerance.

In the aftermath of the global financial crisis, for instance, a survey by the investment management firm MFS showed that young investors—those in their 20s and 30s—were more scared of stocks than near retirees and were keeping as much as a third of their portfolios in cash. At the same time, they held less than half their portfolios in equities, which given their time horizon seemed like an extremely conservative approach.

With a risk-based asset allocation fund, you don't have to worry about decisions when it comes to your individual stock and bond holdings. However, if you select a risk-based fund that is either too conservative or too risky for your circumstances, you may fall short of your financial goals simply based on that error.

Moreover, even if you select the proper asset allocation fund and risk level for you at the moment, your work is still not done. Because the fund will simply rebalance your portfolio back to its original, static mix, the fund will never adjust to changes that take place in your life. If, for instance, after holding an aggressive allocation fund throughout your 20s and 30s, you decide that you'd be more comfortable with a greater weighting in bonds now that you're in your 40s and 50s, it will be up to you to sell out of the aggressive allocation fund and use the proceeds to buy a moderate allocation portfolio.

These funds don't offer the customization that you may be seeking, and they require a level of long-term attention that investors may not realize. If you're looking for more personalization and customization, you may be interested in a different type of asset allocation fund:

Option 3: Target Date Life-Cycle Funds

These are all-in-one portfolios of stocks and bonds that use your age—or your time horizon—to customize a strategy.

What Are They?

Around a decade ago, the mutual fund industry came up with a new type of product that's designed to be truly a one-decision asset allocation fund. These target date funds are easily identified by their odd names with dates at the end. For instance, there's the Vanguard Target Retirement 2045 Fund, the Fidelity Freedom 2035 Fund, the iShares Target Date 2030 Fund, or the T. Rowe Price Retirement 2025 Fund.

The dates, contrary to some misconceptions, do not signify when the funds are set to expire or mature in some way and return investors their money. These funds don't expire or mature. They go on in perpetuity. Rather, the dates are used to peg a time horizon. The Vanguard Target Retirement 2045 Fund, for example, is designed for someone who expects to retire in the year 2045. Traditionally, that would be suited for someone born around 1980 or so who plans to retire and start drawing income at around age 65. The T. Rowe Price Retirement 2025 Fund, on the other hand, is better suited for investors born around 1960.

Though they are often labeled as retirement vehicles—which in fact they are—these funds aren't targeted only to near-retirees or those investors who are already retired. Instead, these funds are designed to be "set it and forget it" portfolios that you can buy at any age, whether you're 20 or 60. How? Unlike risk-based asset allocation funds, whose mix of stocks and bonds remains static over time, target date life-cycle funds are designed to change with you over the course of your own life.

For example, with a T. Rowe Price Retirement target date fund, the portfolio is set to be around 90 percent invested in equities until you are about 15 years away from retirement. At that point, the T. Rowe Price funds will dial down their equity exposure to less than 80 percent. Then within five years of retirement, the funds downshift again to around 65 percent in stocks. At retirement, that falls to 55 percent equities, and then the funds start an even more pronounced decline in aggressiveness that takes your stock weighting down to 45 percent five years into retirement, 35 percent 15 years into retirement, and 25 percent 25 years after you quit work (Table 9-4).

TABLE 9–4 T. Rowe Price's Target Date Glide Path
Here's how one fund reduces risk as investors get older.

Stage of Life	Equity Stake	Bond Stake	Cash Stake
25 years before retirement	90%	10%	1%
15 years before retirement	79%	20%	1%
5 years before retirement	64%	30%	6%
At retirement	55%	35%	10%
5 years into retirement	46%	39%	15%
15 years into retirement	35%	46%	20%
25 years into retirement	26%	54%	20%
30 years into retirement	20%	60%	20%

Source: T. Rowe Price

Advantage 1: No Decision-Making Is Required

For investors who believe in the importance of asset allocation—but who don't believe they have the time or skills to implement the proper strategy at all times—a target date fund offers a decent substitute. For starters, you don't have to decide on anything. Based on your age, you can figure out about when you will turn 65 and then select the appropriate life-cycle fund with a retirement year that's closest to that target.

Along the way, you never have to worry about selecting individual stocks or bonds—or, for that matter, stock mutual funds or bond mutual funds to populate your portfolio based on your asset allocation mix. Nor do you have to monitor any investments (including the target date fund itself) to make sure they remain appropriate for your needs and circumstances.

What's more, you don't have to decide when or how to rebalance the portfolio that's already assembled. That is taken care of for you by the fund manager, who maintains the target date fund's mix of investments based on where the fund is in your life cycle. And when your life circumstances change and your risk tolerance changes, you don't have to affirmatively do anything to ensure that your strategy grows more conservative as you age. That is the beauty of the life-cycle fund.

Finally, the fund—even though it is not customized to you and you alone, but is an off-the-shelf product that is mass marketed—will know generally when you're in that critical window that starts five years before retirement and continues into the first five years of retirement. That's when any major losses in your portfolio can really affect the longevity of your nest egg and your ability to safely draw down adequate income to support your needs after your career is over. Once your life cycle crosses from accumulation to preservation and withdrawal, that's when most life-cycle funds switch from being mostly in equities targeting growth and take a defensive stance that focuses on preservation of capital and the production of income.

Advantage 2: You Can Set It and Forget It

With most financial relationships, the saver or the investor is the one who must instigate change. With an insurance product, for instance, it's up to you to renew the contract annually and to alter the terms from time to time to better reflect your circumstances. With a 401(k) retirement account, you must decide what percentage of your salary to contribute to your plan each year, and as you grow older and as you earn more in salary, you must decide how to gradually increase the contribution amount over time—and how to alter your investments as circumstances change.

Yet a target date fund does not require you to revisit it, which explains why these vehicles have become some of the most popular in terms of drawing new assets. Indeed, throughout the 2000s, when many fund investors had turned their backs on equity-oriented products—and when equity-oriented funds were seeing net redemptions rather than new fund flows—target date funds continued to attract billions of new money and now hold more than half a trillion dollars in investable assets.

Target date funds, in fact, are well suited for 401(k) plans, since these vehicles allow investors who don't have time for or interest in managing their money to set a plan and literally forget to do everything except gradually increase their contribution amounts over time as they start to earn more.

A recent survey by Charles Schwab showed that many 401(k) participants are frustrated by the overwhelming complexity and choices in their plans. According to that survey, the majority of 401(k) investors say that 401(k) investment information is more confusing than their healthcare benefit options, which are notorious for being dizzying. Nearly half—46 percent—say they aren't sure what the best investment options are for them within their plans. And more than one-third say they "feel a lot of stress choosing their 401(k) investment options."

The funny thing is, most 401(k) investors have the answer to those questions and fears within their plans. The vast majority of 401(k) plans—roughly two-thirds, according to the Employee Benefit Research Institute—offer a target date option, and if yours does, it's not a bad choice to use it as a default. In fact, many workplace-sponsored retirement plans that have an automatic enrollment system will default their employees into a target date fund until and unless a worker affirmatively chooses to switch out of that investment option.

Advantage 3: You Can Customize the Funds

Because target date funds are off-the-shelf products, they are not able to truly adhere to an individual investor's needs. Still, there is a simple way for all target date investors to customize their experience with these funds as their circumstances change. For example, say you were born in 1970, with an expectation to retire in 2035. So you go out and invest in the Schwab Target 2035 Fund, with around 80 percent of its assets held in equities. And say you determine that, based on your life circumstances—and your recent experiences in the market—you no longer feel comfortable with such a high exposure to equities.

You can still adhere to a target date approach, but simply swap out the funds. There is nothing contractual that keeps you locked into a target date fund once you start investing. As with any other retail mutual fund or ETF, you can choose to sell out of it and go with a competing company's target date fund. For example, you might decide that you're more comfortable with the equity weighting in the Fidelity Freedom 2035 Fund, which keeps around 70 percent of its assets in stocks and 30 percent in bonds and cash. Or you could stay within the Schwab offering, but decide that instead of the Schwab Target 2035 Fund, you're actually more comfortable going with the Schwab Target 2030 offering, with less than a 75 percent weighting in equities, or even the Schwab Target 2025 Fund, which invests roughly two-thirds of its money in equities, reserving the rest for bonds and cash.

Here's another common scenario: Say you were born in 1970 and had every expectation of retiring by age 65, in the year 2035. But let's assume that by the time you turned 40, you realized that your health wasn't as strong as you thought it would be. In that case, the notion of being able to keep working until you're 65 may seem fairly remote. In that case, there is nothing wrong with swapping out of the 2035 target date fund that you're currently in and swapping into a 2030 or 2025 portfolio.

Conversely, if you're cruising along in your 40s, your health is good, and you come to the realization that you want to work well past age 65, you can just as easily grow more aggressive with your target date funds. You can do so by switching from that original 2035 choice to a 2040 or 2045 offering. In the case of the Schwab target date funds, the Schwab Target 2040 portfolio maintains an equity weighting of around 85 percent, which is about five percentage points more aggressive than the 2035 fund.

What Are the Shortcomings?

Problem 1: There Is No Consensus on What the Glide Path Should Be

The ability to customize your own target date strategy—by selecting different strategies offered by different fund companies—highlights a big problem with target date funds: No two companies can seem to agree when it comes to what a person's asset allocation ought to be at every stage of life (Figure 9-2). In the parlance of the mutual fund industry, this is referred to as the target date fund's "glide path," or the steps through which a target date fund downshifts from being extremely aggressive to increasingly conservative.

For example, while many different target date providers may assume that a 20-something should have 90 percent or more of his or her money in equities, there is no shortage of opinions on how that equity exposure should be ratcheted back as that investor hits his or her 30s and 40s and beyond.

The T. Rowe Price Retirement 2040 Fund, for example, invests more than 90 percent of its assets in equities, which means that the firm believes that a 35-year-old ought to be extremely aggressive. By comparison, the Schwab Target 2040 Fund keeps around 85 percent of its money invested in stocks. The Vanguard Target Retirement 2040 Fund takes you to around 80 percent in equities. To further confuse matters, T. Rowe Price now offers a slightly more conservative set of target date funds as a second option to its original set of funds, and the T. Rowe Price Target Retire 2040 Advisor Fund keeps about 75 percent in equities. Meanwhile, the Fidelity Freedom 2040 Fund is around 75 percent in stocks.

The glide path issue becomes even more serious at retirement. A recent survey by the Securities and Exchange Commission found that a majority of target date fund owners expect that at their retirement, their target date funds would hold 40 percent or less in equities. Yet the T. Rowe Price Retirement 2015 Fund, meant for folks who are just at retirement, maintains a 60 percent weighting to equities. The Vanguard Target Retirement 2015 Fund is closer to 50 percent stocks. And the T. Rowe Price Target Retire 2015 Advisor Fund, the Fidelity Freedom Fund 2015, and the Schwab Target 2015 Fund all are at 45 percent stocks. All the way at the other end of the spectrum is the MFS Lifetime 2015 Fund, which at retirement keeps only about 30 percent in equities, with 60 percent in fixed income and around 10 percent in cash.

Problem 2: These Funds Aren't Properly Understood

Despite the widespread availability of target date funds in 401(k)s—and the growing popularity of these all-in-one products in and outside of retirement plans—the fact remains that they are generally misunderstood by the investing public. Among the major misconceptions:

Myth: Many investors incorrectly believe that the target date that's listed on the fund points to the date at which the fund expires. Again, these funds do not mature or expire as a bond does.

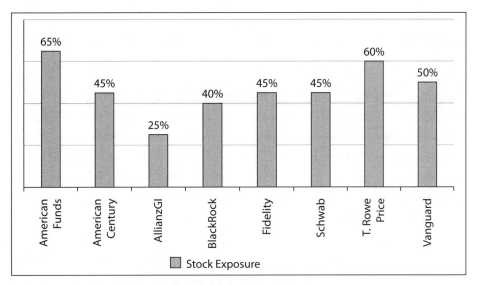

FIGURE 9-2 Variations on a Theme
These 2015 target date funds all have differing exposure to equities.
Source: Morningstar

Myth: Many investors incorrectly believe that the target date that's listed on the fund points to the date at which the fund becomes most conservative in its allocation strategy. In other words, the belief is that after the retirement date is reached, the fund ceases to glide further down. Yet in reality, these funds continue to reduce their aggressiveness years and decades after the date. Case in point: The T. Rowe Price retirement funds will gradually dial down to as little as 20 percent equities 30 years past the target retirement year. Many of these funds continue to ratchet down gradually, as the life expectancy of folks who make it into retirement is growing so long.

Myth: Many investors still believe that these funds offer guaranteed income. In fact, even among investors who own shares of a target date retirement fund, about two in five falsely believe that in the year in which the target date is reached, the fund will start paying the investor a guaranteed income, according to a recent survey about target date funds conducted by the Securities and Exchange Commission.

Myth: Target date funds with the same target year in their names will invest money in the same way. Roughly half of investors surveyed seem to think that target date funds are like commodities—that each target date fund with 2020 in its name will act and function the same way. As has already been discussed, nothing could be further from the truth.

Problem 3: These Funds Don't Have a Good Track Record of Reducing Risk

Surveys indicate that the biggest reason why investors opt for a target date fund isn't necessarily simplicity, but rather the perceived sense of safety that these funds foster. One recent survey showed that while about one-third of target date fund users chose these vehicles due to their instant diversification and relative simplicity, more than two out of five favored target dates because they viewed them as inherently safe investments (Figure 9-3).

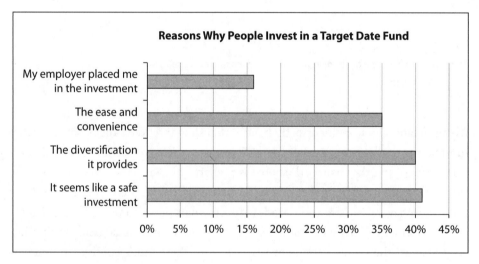

FIGURE 9-3 Reasons Why People Use Target Date Funds
Simplicity and safety drive the decision to invest in target date portfolios.
Source: SEC

Yet in the most recent bear market, where safety was in demand, many traditional target date funds failed to prevent big losses for shareholders who were near or at retirement. For example, many of these portfolios with a 2010 in their names—meaning they were designed for folks who, in 2008, were just two years away from retiring—fell between 25 percent and 30 percent in value because most still had half or more of their assets in equities. Some funds lost considerably more. A portfolio managed by Oppenheimer funds tumbled nearly 45 percent.

Problem 4: You Have to Know How to Use It

This may seem like a silly thing to say. After all, it's been argued that these are "no-decision" or "one-decision" vehicles. But no matter how you get started with a target date fund—whether you voluntarily pick one or whether it is temporarily selected for you by your plan—it is important to know how to use it. If you do use it, do so properly.

These funds are meant to be used as the sole fund in your investment portfolio, not in a core and explore manner. By combining the target date fund with other static funds, you will inadvertently redirect the guide path intended by the fund manager. Yet the reality is that just a minority of retirement-oriented investors use these funds in the proper manner.

For example, an SEC study found that only 9 percent of investors who use target date funds keep all of their investable assets in the fund. On the other hand, a majority—51 percent—keep less than half their portfolios in these funds, presumably investing the rest on their own or through advisors. If that's the case, there's a good chance that they could be upsetting their own asset allocation strategy without even knowing it.

QUIZ

1. **Balanced funds are just as diversified as asset allocation funds.**
    A. True
    B. False

2. **Risk-based asset allocation funds require you to ...**
    A. Select your level of aggressiveness.
    B. Rebalance your strategy.
    C. Select your glide path.

3. **All asset allocation funds put your investment strategy on a glide path.**
    A. True
    B. False

4. **Balanced funds are likely to have how much exposure to equities?**
    A. 40 percent
    B. 60 percent
    C. 80 percent
    D. None

5. **Conservative risk asset allocation funds are likely to have as much in equities as balanced funds.**
    A. True
    B. False

6. **Target date retirement funds are designed to return your principal to you at a certain date.**
    A. True
    B. False

7. **The year listed in a target date retirement fund represents the point at which ...**
    A. You plan to retire.
    B. The fund hands you back your money.
    C. The fund falls to its lowest equity allocation.
    D. The fund converts to all bonds and cash.

8. **Moderate risk target date funds all adhere to the same glide path.**
    A. True
    B. False

9. **Which of the following types of all-in-one funds is meant to be used in a core and explore fashion?**
    A. Target date funds
    B. Risk-based asset allocation funds
    C. Balanced funds

10. **Once set in motion, you should never switch out of one target date fund into another.**
    A. True
    B. False

Final Exam

1. **Which of these investors needs to pay attention to asset allocation?**
   A. Individual investors
   B. Individual investors who aren't skilled at picking stocks and bonds
   C. Professional investors
   D. All of the above
   E. None of the above

2. **Which of these factors influence your asset allocation strategy?**
   A. Your age
   B. Your investing skill level
   C. Your past performance as an investor

3. **Asset allocation is nearly as important as individual security selection.**
   A. True
   B. False

4. **Asset allocation is a form of controlling ...**
   A. Your risk.
   B. Your returns.
   C. Both.
   D. Neither.

5. **In establishing an appropriate asset allocation for you, which of the following should influence your decisions?**
   A. Your emotions
   B. Your net worth
   C. Neither
   D. Both

6. **The richer you are, the less you should be in stocks because you don't need capital appreciation.**
   A. True
   B. False

7. **The poorer you are, the less you should be in stocks because you can't afford to lose what little you have.**
   A. True
   B. False

8. **If you are adept at selecting individual stocks and bonds, you don't need to worry about asset allocation.**
   A. True
   B. False

9. **The more time you have to invest, the less you need ...**
   A. Stocks.
   B. Bonds.
   C. An asset allocation plan.

10. **The less you time you have to invest, the more you need ...**
    A. Stocks.
    B. Bonds.
    C. An asset allocation plan.

11. **An asset allocation plan helps you defeat ...**
    A. A bear market.
    B. Recession.
    C. Inflation.

12. **Which of the following are ingredients that contribute to investing success?**
    A. Investment selection
    B. Investment timing
    C. Asset allocation
    D. All of the above
    E. None of the above

13. **Which of these strategies works hand-in-glove with asset allocation?**
    A. Diversification
    B. Concentration
    C. Market timing

14. **It is impossible to predict how various asset classes will perform over the long run.**
    A. True
    B. False

15. **Stocks make more money over time than bonds, but they ...**
    A. Often lose more than bonds in the short run.
    B. Provide ballast to your portfolio.
    C. Offer guaranteed income.

16. **Bonds are useful because they ...**
    A. Guarantee that you won't lose money on your investment.
    B. Are assured of outpacing inflation.
    C. Provide a consistent source of income.
    D. Deliver growing dividends over time.

17. **Economic growth in a particular market is correlated with that market's future ...**
    A. Stock performance.
    B. Bond performance.
    C. Both.
    D. Neither.

18. **Over a short time period, which of the following is good at predicting stock market performance?**
    A. Valuations
    B. Corporate earnings
    C. Economic growth
    D. None of the above
    E. All of the above

19. **Reversion to the mean refers to the fact that investments …**
    A. Immediately revert to their historic performance.
    B. Usually revert to their historic performance.
    C. Eventually revert to their historic performance.
    D. None of the above.

20. **Stocks have beaten bonds in …**
    A. 50 percent of calendar years in history.
    B. 60 percent of calendar years in history.
    C. 70 percent of calendar years in history.
    D. 90 percent of calendar years in history.

21. **Stocks have beaten bonds in …**
    A. More than 50 percent of rolling 20-year periods in history.
    B. More than 60 percent of rolling 20-year periods in history.
    C. More than 70 percent of rolling 20-year periods in history.
    D. More than 90 percent of rolling 20-year periods in history.

22. **Different asset classes take turns leading the market every …**
    A. Year.
    B. 20 years.
    C. They never take turns.

23. **In the long run, to earn the biggest returns, you must …**
    A. Expose your portfolio to risk.
    B. Expose your portfolio to income.
    C. Expose your portfolio to capital appreciation.

24. **Asset allocation assumes that diversification works ...**
    A. All of the time.
    B. Most of the time.
    C. Never.

25. **In a financial crisis, most asset classes are expected to move in ...**
    A. Greater correlation.
    B. Less correlation.
    C. The same correlation.

26. **If two asset classes move in the same direction, holding both has no diversification benefit.**
    A. True
    B. False

27. **The increasing globalization of the world's economies means that asset allocation is ...**
    A. Less important.
    B. More important.
    C. Just as important.

28. **If one asset class has a correlation of 1.0 with another, that means that it moves ...**
    A. In the same direction as the other.
    B. In lockstep with the other.
    C. In the exact opposite direction from the other.

29. **Which of the following is a measure of risk?**
    A. Standard deviation
    B. Sharpe ratio
    C. Volatility

30. **Beta measures how volatile an investment is relative to ...**
    A. Its historic average.
    B. Similar investments.
    C. The broad market.

31. **Standard deviation measures how volatile an investment is relative to ...**
    A. Its historic average.
    B. Similar investments.
    C. The broad market.

32. **Equities provide investors with ...**
    A. Capital appreciation.
    B. Income.
    C. Both.
    D. Neither.

33. **Bonds provide investors with ...**
    A. Capital appreciation.
    B. Income.
    C. Both.
    D. Neither.

34. **Stocks are important because they offer you exposure to ...**
    A. Growth.
    B. Income.
    C. Volatility.

35. **Bonds are important because they offer you ...**
    A. Guarantees against losses.
    B. Guarantees of stability.
    C. Guarantees of income.

36. **Bonds are riskless assets.**
    A. True
    B. False

37. **Treasury bonds are riskless assets.**
    A. True
    B. False

38. **If small stocks deliver greater long-term returns than large caps, why not just invest in small-company shares?**
    A. Small caps are more expensive.
    B. Small caps are more volatile.
    C. Small caps offer less income.

39. **Which of these stocks are supposed to anchor your portfolio?**
   A. Large caps
   B. Small caps
   C. Foreign

40. **Large stocks make up what percent of the total U.S. equity market?**
   A. 25 percent
   B. 50 percent
   C. 65 percent
   D. 80 percent

41. **The "growth" in growth stocks represents ...**
   A. Faster earnings growth.
   B. Faster total return growth.
   C. Faster income growth.

42. **The higher a stock's price/earnings ratio, the cheaper the shares are.**
   A. True
   B. False

43. **The "value" in value stocks represents ...**
   A. The value of the company's assets on its balance sheet.
   B. The relative market value applied to the company.
   C. Both.
   D. Neither.

44. **Growth stocks are usually found in ...**
   A. The technology sector.
   B. The utility sector.
   C. Both.
   D. Neither.

45. **Value stocks are usually found in ...**
   A. The technology sector.
   B. The utility sector.
   C. Both.
   D. Neither.

46. **Growth stocks tend to outperform value stocks in the long run.**
    A. True
    B. False

47. **Value stocks tend to outperform growth stocks in the long run.**
    A. True
    B. False

48. **Because of their size, large stocks tend to outperform smaller shares.**
    A. True
    B. False

49. **Because small stocks are worth less than large ones, these stocks have less room to fall.**
    A. True
    B. False

50. **The "small" in small stocks refers to ...**
    A. Profits.
    B. Book value.
    C. Market value.
    D. Price.

51. **Small stocks are ...**
    A. Less risky than large stocks.
    B. Just as risky as large stocks.
    C. More risky than large stocks.

52. **Small stocks represent what percent of the U.S. market?**
    A. 0 to 10 percent
    B. 10 to 20 percent
    C. 20 to 30 percent
    D. 30 to 40 percent
    E. 50 percent or more

53. **Foreign stocks make up what percent of the total global stock market?**
    A. 0 to 10 percent
    B. 10 to 20 percent
    C. 20 to 30 percent
    D. 30 to 40 percent
    E. 50 percent or more

54. **Because many U.S. companies do a good deal of business in Europe, Asia, and Latin America, you don't need added foreign exposure.**
    A. True
    B. False

55. **Developed market foreign stocks and emerging market stocks are …**
    A. Two separate asset classes.
    B. The same asset class.
    C. Two variations of the same asset class.

56. **Emerging market stocks include shares of companies based in China, the second largest economy in the world. So emerging market stocks tend to be …**
    A. More important than developed foreign market stocks.
    B. Less important than developed foreign market stocks.
    C. Faster growing than foreign developed market shares.
    D. Slower growing than foreign developed market shares.

57. **Bonds provide which of the following to your portfolio?**
    A. Ballast
    B. Income
    C. Diversification
    D. All of the above
    E. None of the above

58. **Government bonds are risk-free assets.**
    A. True
    B. False

59. **Corporate bonds return more than government bonds over the long run because ...**
    A. They currently yield more than government bonds.
    B. They currently yield less than government bonds.
    C. They expose investors to more risk than do government bonds.
    D. They expose investors to less risk than do government bonds.

60. **When stocks rise, bonds ...**
    A. Always rise.
    B. Sometimes rise.
    C. Always fall.
    D. Sometimes fall.
    E. B and D.

61. **The longer your time horizon, the greater your need for ...**
    A. Stocks.
    B. Bonds.
    C. Cash.
    D. Inflation.

62. **The shorter your time horizon, the less you need ...**
    A. Stocks.
    B. Bonds.
    C. Cash.
    D. Inflation.

63. **The more time you have to invest, the more you can afford to ...**
    A. Play it safe.
    B. Avoid investing entirely.
    C. Take risks.

64. **The 100-minus rule has limitations, but it at least conveys the notion that your asset allocation plan must get ...**
    A. Gradually more aggressive over time.
    B. Gradually more conservative over time.
    C. Rapidly more aggressive over time.
    D. Rapidly more conservative over time.

65. **Younger investors can afford to take more risks with their portfolios because they ...**
    A. Have more time.
    B. Have an income to offset potential losses.
    C. Are emotionally more resilient.
    D. All of the above.
    E. None of the above.

66. **One problem with numbers-based asset allocation strategies like the 100-minus rule is that they ...**
    A. Fail to account for emotions and preferences.
    B. Fail to stop growing conservative over time.
    C. Are too aggressive.

67. **An 80 percent stock / 20 percent bond portfolio is considered ...**
    A. Conservative.
    B. Moderate.
    C. Aggressive.
    D. Dangerous.

68. **An 80 percent stock / 20 percent bond portfolio has ...**
    A. About a 25 percent chance of losing money in any calendar year.
    B. About a 25 percent chance of losing money over any 5-year period.
    C. A 10 percent chance of losing money in any calendar year.

69. **The worst one-year loss for a 60 percent stock / 40 percent bond portfolio was ...**
    A. Twice as big as the losses for a 100 percent stock portfolio.
    B. Half as big as the losses for a 100 percent stock portfolio.
    C. The same as the losses for a 100 percent bond portfolio.

70. **A 50 percent stock / 50 percent bond portfolio has ...**
    A. Never lost money in any calendar year.
    B. Never lost money in any 5-year stretch.
    C. Never lost money in any 10-year stretch.

71. **A 30 percent stock / 50 percent bond portfolio has never lost money over any five-year stretch in history.**
    A. True
    B. False

72. **A 30 percent stock / 70 percent bond portfolio has never lost money in any calendar year.**
    A. True
    B. False

73. **Strategic asset allocation refers to ...**
    A. Your short-term investment strategy.
    B. Your long-term investment strategy.
    C. Your short-term trading strategy.

74. **Tactical asset allocation refers to ...**
    A. Your short-term investment strategy.
    B. Your long-term investment strategy.
    C. Your short-term trading strategy.

75. **Tactical asset allocation requires investors to ...**
    A. Undo their strategic allocations.
    B. Go against their strategic allocations.
    C. Neither.

76. **You can make tactical shifts in your portfolio by ...**
    A. Changing your weighting in broad asset classes.
    B. Changing your subasset classes.
    C. Both.
    D. Neither.

77. **Adjusting your portfolio through subasset classes does not change the risk-reward profile of your portfolio.**
    A. True
    B. False

78. **Which of the following strategies represents a common portfolio "tilt"?**
    A. Value
    B. Core and explore
    C. Total bond market

79. **Value stocks outperform because they are ...**
    A. Higher priced by nature.
    B. Overlooked.
    C. They don't outperform.

80. **Small-cap stocks expose you to greater risk. Therefore you should tilt away from them.**
    A. True
    B. False

81. **Low-volatility stocks tend to have lower ...**
    A. Returns.
    B. Standard deviation.
    C. Beta.

82. **Low-volatility stocks are lower risk. They deliver ...**
    A. Lower returns than the broad market.
    B. The same returns as the broad market.
    C. Higher returns than the broad market.

83. **Which of the following is considered an inflation hedge?**
    A. Commodities
    B. Stocks
    C. TIPs bonds
    D. All of the above
    E. None of the above

84. **Tactical portfolio tilts are limited to long-term market inefficiencies.**
    A. True
    B. False

85. **If you are seeking to boost income, a natural place to turn is ...**
    A. Bonds.
    B. Dividend-paying stocks.
    C. REITs.
    D. All of the above.
    E. None of the above.

86. **Income is the only reason to own cash.**
    A. True
    B. False

87. **High-yielding dividend-paying stocks are riskier than dividend growers.**
    A. True
    B. False

88. **Rebalancing is a technique to ...**
    A. Maximize your gains.
    B. Maximize your risks.
    C. Maintain your gains.
    D. Maintain your risk.

89. **If you failed to rebalance in the late 1990s, your 60 percent stock / 40 percent bond allocation would have turned into ...**
    A. 40 percent stocks / 60 percent bonds.
    B. 50 percent stocks / 50 percent bonds.
    C. 80 percent stocks / 20 percent bonds.

90. **If you fail to rebalance and your portfolio loses 50 percent of its value, how much would your portfolio have to gain to break even?**
    A. 25 percent
    B. 50 percent
    C. 75 percent
    D. 100 percent

91. **If you fail to rebalance and your portfolio loses 60 percent of its value, how much would your portfolio have to gain to break even?**
    A. 75 percent
    B. 100 percent
    C. 125 percent
    D. 150 percent

92. **If you are a "buy and hold" investor, you should not rebalance.**
    A. True
    B. False

93. **Routinely rebalancing your stock exposure is important because bear markets typically materialize every ...**
    A. 3 years.
    B. 5 years.
    C. 10 years.
    D. 25 years.

94. **Rebalancing will make you more money than not rebalancing ...**
    A. All of the time
    B. None of the time
    C. Some of the time

95. **Which method of rebalancing makes you the most money?**
    A. Time-based
    B. Threshold-based
    C. Neither

96. **A major reason not to rebalance too frequently is that ...**
    A. It's costly.
    B. It's risky.
    C. It's complicated.

97. **When you rebalance, you ...**
    A. Buy low and sell high.
    B. Buy high and sell low.
    C. Sell your losers.
    D. Buy winners.

98. **Rebalancing may not boost returns, but it definitely ...**
    A. Reduces costs.
    B. Reduces volatility.
    C. Increases volatility.

99. **Rebalancing is ultimately a ...**
    A. Value strategy.
    B. Growth strategy.
    C. Large-cap strategy.

100. **While rebalancing requires you to sell some of your winning assets, you can still sell the poorest performers among your winning asset class.**
    A. True
    B. False

Answers to Quizzes and Final Exam

Chapter 1	Chapter 3	Chapter 5	Chapter 7
1. **A**	1. **C**	1. **A**	1. **D**
2. **C**	2. **B**	2. **A**	2. **B**
3. **B**	3. **B**	3. **C**	3. **A**
4. **A**	4. **B**	4. **C**	4. **A**
5. **C**	5. **A**	5. **A**	5. **D**
6. **A**	6. **C**	6. **B**	6. **A**
7. **C**	7. **A**	7. **A**	7. **C**
8. **C**	8. **A**	8. **D**	8. **A**
9. **E**	9. **D**	9. **C**	9. **B**
10. **A**	10. **C**	10. **D**	10. **A**

Chapter 2	Chapter 4	Chapter 6	Chapter 8
1. **C**	1. **B**	1. **C**	1. **D**
2. **A**	2. **C**	2. **B**	2. **C**
3. **B**	3. **B**	3. **B**	3. **D**
4. **D**	4. **A**	4. **D**	4. **B**
5. **C**	5. **A**	5. **C**	5. **C**
6. **A**	6. **B**	6. **A**	6. **C**
7. **B**	7. **A**	7. **C**	7. **A**
8. **C**	8. **B**	8. **A**	8. **B**
9. **C**	9. **B**	9. **B**	9. **A**
10. **B**	10. **A**	10. **B**	10. **B**

Chapter 9
1. B
2. A
3. B
4. B
5. B
6. B
7. A
8. B
9. C
10. B

Final Exam
1. D
2. A
3. B
4. C
5. D
6. B
7. B
8. B
9. B
10. B
11. C
12. D
13. A
14. B
15. A
16. C
17. D
18. D
19. C
20. B
21. D
22. A
23. A
24. B
25. A
26. B
27. C
28. B
29. A
30. C
31. A
32. C
33. C
34. A
35. C
36. B
37. B
38. B
39. A
40. D
41. A
42. B
43. B
44. A
45. B
46. B
47. A
48. B
49. B
50. C
51. C
52. B
53. E
54. B
55. C
56. C
57. D
58. B
59. C
60. E
61. A
62. A
63. C
64. B
65. D
66. A
67. C
68. A
69. B
70. C
71. A
72. B
73. B
74. A
75. C
76. C
77. B
78. A
79. B
80. B
81. C
82. C
83. D
84. B
85. D
86. B
87. A
88. D
89. C
90. D
91. D
92. B
93. B
94. C
95. C
96. A
97. A
98. B
99. A
100. A

Index